LAND HEIGHTS
AND OCEAN DEPTHS

meters		feet
3000		9842
2000		6562
1000		3281
500		1640
200		656
sea level		sea level
		LAND BELOW SEA LEVEL
200		656
3000		9842
6000		19685

0   50   100   150   200   250   300   350   400 Miles

0   100   200   300   400   500   600 Kilometers

Manitoba

ANTHONY HOCKING

Publisher: John Rae

Managing Editor: Robin Brass

Manuscript Editor: Jocelyn Van Huyse

Production Supervisor: Lynda Rhodes

Graphics: Pirjo Selistemagi

Cover: Brian F. Reynolds

THE CANADA SERIES

McGraw-Hill Ryerson Limited

Toronto   Montreal   New York   St. Louis   San Francisco
Auckland   Bogotá   Düsseldorf   Johannesburg   London
Madrid   Mexico   New Delhi   Panama   Paris   São Paulo
Singapore   Sydney   Tokyo

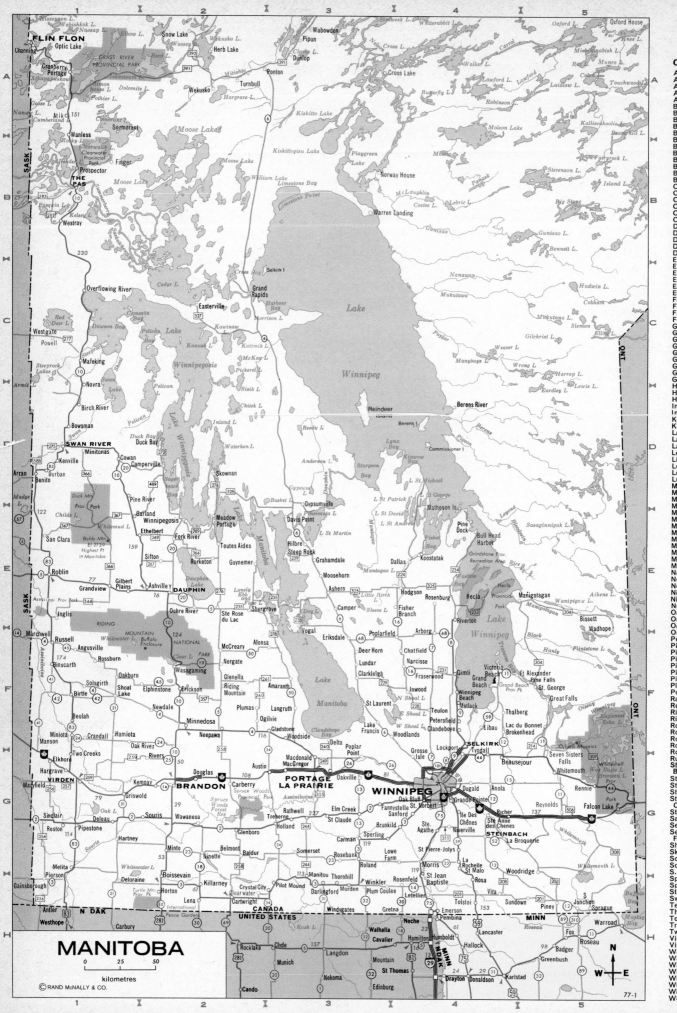

MANITOBA

MANITOBA

Population: 986,000
(1971 estimate)

Capital: Winnipeg

Cities and Towns

77-1

CONTENTS

MANITOBA

Manitoba is middle Canada, the keystone province that links east with west. It is located nearly as far from the Pacific as it is from the Atlantic, even though it possesses more than 600 km of saltwater coastline along the shores of Hudson Bay.

Many Canadians think of Manitoba as a prairie province, as if it contained little but featureless plains. However, the plains occupy only two-fifths of its area, while most of the remainder is part of Canada's Precambrian Shield. The forest wilderness of northern and eastern Manitoba is in startling contrast with the ordered wheatlands of the south and west.

Even more remarkable are Manitoba's water resources. Following the last Ice Age, most of the province was submerged by the prehistoric 'Lake Agassiz,' and remnants of it survive in Lake Winnipeg and its smaller neighbours, Lakes Manitoba and Winnipegosis. Great rivers like the Churchill and Nelson race to Hudson Bay, and northern Manitoba holds so many lakes that they have never been counted.

Water gives Manitoba its name. The precise origin of the term is uncertain, but Indians associated it with the rapids in the narrows of Lake Manitoba. To them, the rapids were the voice of their great spirit Manitou. At the request of Louis Riel's Métis, 'Manitoba' was the name given to the province in 1870 when it joined Confederation.

The Métis founded Manitoba, together with the British and Canadian colonists of the Red river settlement established by Lord Selkirk in 1811. Between 1874 and 1914 the early arrivals were joined by tens of thousands of settlers from Russia, Iceland, Poland, and many other countries who gave Manitoba an ethnic diversity unsurpassed in Canada.

Among Manitoba's assets are rich soil, minerals, forests, and immense hydroelectric power. All these are important, but they are overshadowed by human qualities — the close family loyalties, community tolerance, and neighbourhood spirit that make the keystone province 'Friendly Manitoba.'

Passing aspens on the shoreline, canoeists glide through the clear waters of a lake in Whiteshell provincial park, eastern Manitoba.

At first glimpse, tundra of the Churchill region on the shores of Hudson Bay appears barren. A closer look reveals a myriad of tiny flowers that make northern Manitoba a botanist's paradise.

The O'Hanley river, east of Lake Winnipeg, cuts into the hard rock of the Canadian Shield, which comprises about half of Manitoba's surface area.

SHIELD AND SEDIMENT

Manitoba's topography is comparatively level, rising slowly from the shores of Hudson Bay towards the south and west. Its geology is more complex, a core of Precambrian bedrock overlain by sediments both to south-west and to north-east.

Precambrian rock was so named by pioneer geologists who could find no trace of fossils in it. The earliest rocks in which they discovered fossils were dated to the Cambrian era, beginning about 400 million years ago. Rock without fossils was dismissed as Precambrian, meaning that its age could not be determined.

Since then, techniques have been developed to analyze Precambrian deposits. One of them is radiometric dating, which gauges the rate of decay of certain materials in rocks. Using this technique, geologists have recognized significant differences between 'provinces' of Canada's Precambrian Shield.

These differences represent major upheavals or orogenies, the result of stresses within the earth's crust. Two of the upheavals affected Manitoba. The earlier, the Kenoran orogeny, occurred about 2.6 billion years ago. It took place in Superior province, east of the Nelson river and stretching into what is now Ontario.

The later upheaval, known as the Hudsonian, occurred about 1.7 billion years ago. Its most profound impact was in Churchill province, which starts at the Nelson river and sweeps northward to the Arctic.

Each of the Shield's provinces consists of a jumble of rocks formed over billions of years. The original igneous lava cooled and was eroded by wind and water, creating layers of sedimentation. In many instances, both igneous and sedimentary deposits were metamorphosed under great heat and pressure to create yet more formations.

The Shield contains the bulk of Manitoba's mineral wealth. Around

Rocks of the Precambrian Shield underlie the whole of Manitoba, but in the south and near Hudson Bay they are overlain by sediments.

Thompson, nickel is found in a belt of rocks dipping steeply to a depth of over 160 km. Nearer Flin Flon there are significant reserves of copper and zinc. Small deposits of gold have been found, and in the south-east is one of Canada's few commercial deposits of tantalum.

Towards the south-west, the Precambrian Shield tilts downwards under successive layers of post-Cambrian rock. Ordovician deposits cradle Lake Winnipeg. Silurian, Devonian, and Jurassic rocks hold Lakes Manitoba and Winnipegosis. The Ordovician and Silurian deposits are matched by similar formations beyond the Shield in the Hudson Bay lowlands.

When first laid down, each layer of sediment covered much more of the Shield than it does today. The layers formed on the bottoms of ancient seas, and when the land rose above the waters they were worn away by the forces of erosion — wind, water, frost, and the motion of glaciers.

Crossing south-western Manitoba from Porcupine Mountain to Pembina, passing west of Lakes Manitoba and Winnipegosis, is the drift of the Manitoba Escarpment. Formed of hard Cretaceous shale and sandstone, the uplands west of the escarpment are younger than formations to the east, and have suffered less from erosion.

Far below the Cretaceous rocks, sandwiched between Jurassic and Devonian formations, is a layer of Mississippian rock which holds the oil of the Virden fields. The Mississippian formations do not outcrop in Manitoba, but are the legacy of yet another ancient sea that once washed the prairies.

More recently, all Manitoba was affected by the final Ice Age of the Pleistocene era. A sheet of ice up to two kilometres thick pushed south across the Shield and the plains beyond, scraping soil and vegetation before it, and damming the course of northward-flowing rivers.

So was formed Lake Agassiz, which existed for many thousands of years and changed its boundaries in response to advances and retreats of the glacier. At

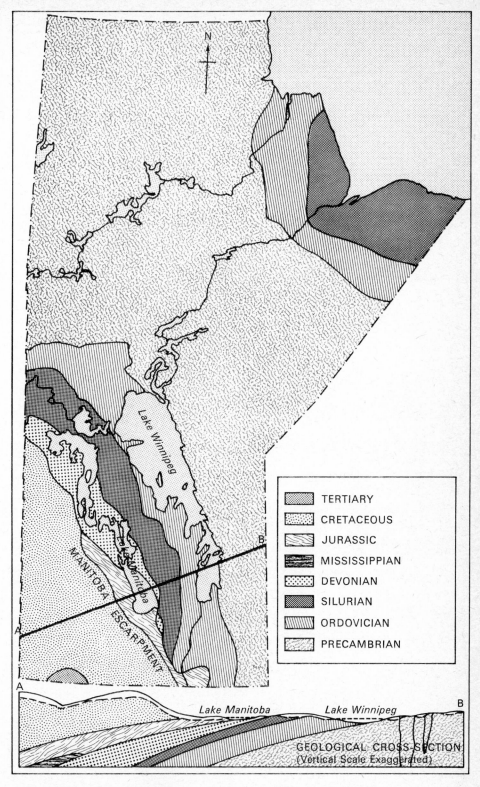

TERTIARY
CRETACEOUS
JURASSIC
MISSISSIPPIAN
DEVONIAN
SILURIAN
ORDOVICIAN
PRECAMBRIAN

Lake Winnipeg

MANITOBA ESCARPMENT

A — A

B — B

Lake Manitoba   Lake Winnipeg

GEOLOGICAL CROSS-SECTION
(Vertical Scale Exaggerated)

one time or another, the lake covered more than half the surface of the province, but never all at one time.

Quantities of rich gumbo deposited in Lake Agassiz are the basis of much of the richest agricultural land in Manitoba. The lake left its mark in a series of beaches which can still be traced, particularly along the line of the Manitoba Escarpment. To date, 55 such beaches

have been recognized.

The enormous weight of the glacier depressed the surface of the land, and the bedrock is still slowly rebounding. The Hudson Bay lowlands remained below sea level for many centuries after the final retreat of the ice, and the coastline was once 250 km inland of where it is now. Marine clays and beach ridges survive to tell the tale.

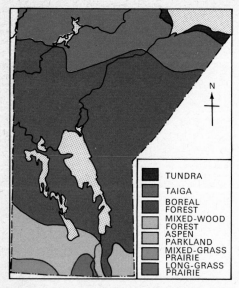

From mixed-grass prairie on high ground in the south-west to tundra on the coast of Hudson Bay, Manitoba displays an entrancing diversity of natural vegetation.

GRASS ROOTS

A century ago, Manitoba contained three distinct zones of vegetation. There was grassland south and west of its great lakes. There was taiga and tundra in the north and north-west. The remainder was forest, most of it boreal.

The tundra has survived intact, and the boreal forest is much as it was, in spite of logging operations. The original prairie, however, has all but disappeared. Wheat grows where prairie flowers bloomed in millions, and sunflowers and rapeseed have supplanted giant bluestem and needle grass.

Prairie (meadow) was the name given to the central plains by early French travellers, who were no doubt delighted with its waving grasses and richly scented flowers after weeks of difficult travel through the eastern forests. Long-grass prairie stretched from Manitoba to Texas.

The long grass — particularly giant bluestem — frequently reached heights of four metres, taller than a man on a horse. It was interspersed with needle grass and sloughgrass, and grew on the deep, rich, black gumbo deposited on the bottom of Lake Agassiz, the area that today constitutes Manitoba's prime agricultural land.

In the far south-west, above the Manitoba Escarpment, soil is shallow and the climate is more arid. There, grasses were shorter, and more species were found. Plant scientists refer to the area as 'mixed-grass prairie,' linking it with the grassland of Saskatchewan and Alberta.

Grasses survived where trees could not because of their superior root systems, often reaching three metres into the soil. Forbs — broad-leafed plants bearing colourful flowers — reach even farther. Any trees hardy enough to survive in the grasslands were eventually destroyed by fire.

Much of what used to be aspen parkland — grassland punctuated by groves of aspen poplar and 'Manitoba maple,' or box elder — has been ploughed. This is particularly the case in the region between the big lakes. In the west, however, aspen poplars are found south of their original range, chiefly because grass fires have been less frequent since the spread of settlement.

In Manitoba's south-east there is a region of mixed forest containing both coniferous and deciduous trees, connected with the mixed forest zone extending through Ontario and Quebec. Eastern white cedar and white and red pine are prominent. Farther north begins the boreal forest, largely consisting of black and white spruce and jack pine.

Still farther north, jack pine is rarer, and black spruce is dominant. Deciduous trees like elm, oak, ash, and birch are found in river valleys. In the taiga or sub-arctic zone there are stands of tamarack and stunted arctic willow. On the shores of Hudson Bay are treeless

The spring break-up in Manitoba's northland, not far from Thompson. Winter snows dissolve into streams and rivers that drain into Hudson Bay.

Manitoba's most impressive cascade, the Pisew Falls on the Grass river, south of Thompson. Around the falls are boreal conifers like those exploited by Manitoba's forest industries.

tundra plains supporting lichen moss, sedge grass, and low-shrub plant communities.

All told, forests cover 63 per cent of Manitoba, but only the southern forests are harvested by forest industries. In the north, the forests are the domain of trappers and remote mining operations and of the increasing numbers of wilderness fishing camps.

The north is the region holding many thousands of Manitoba's lakes, so many that most have never been named, let alone explored. Some are of considerable size, yet even so they are dwarfed by the giants of the south. Lake Winnipeg is the world's thirteenth largest body of fresh water, only slightly smaller than Lake Erie.

Manitoba's lakes are part of a complex drainage system comprising much of North America's interior. From the west comes the Saskatchewan river, which drains much of the region stretching to the Rocky Mountains. It enters Lake Winnipeg by way of The Pas and Cedar Lake.

Also from the west, the Assiniboine collects the water of its tributary, the Souris, then enters the Red river at Winnipeg. The Red river comes from the south and carries the water of the Pembina, which it delivers to Lake Winnipeg. The Winnipeg river drains Lake of the Woods in the east, and enters Lake Winnipeg below Pine Falls.

Lake Winnipegosis empties into Lake Manitoba through the Waterhen river. Lake Manitoba drains into Lake Winnipeg by way of the Dauphin river. Lake Winnipeg flows north down the Nelson river, which travels across the Shield to Hudson Bay. The Nelson runs parallel with the Churchill river to the north, which carries water from the lakes of northern Saskatchewan, and the Hayes river to the east.

Most of the prairies' natural vegetation was ploughed up to make farmland, but some examples survive to display its diversity. These grasses and flowers are typical of the mixed-grass prairie encountered in western Manitoba.

Climate

Situated close to the geographic heart of North America, Manitoba has a 'land controlled' climate with extreme seasonal temperature changes. Winters are cold and clear, summers hot and sunny.

Most of the annual precipitation takes the form of brief but sometimes heavy summer showers. Manitoba receives more rain than either Saskatchewan or Alberta, particularly in the area south of its large lakes. The uplands in the south-western corner tend to be drier than the rest of the province.

Snow falls heavily in all parts of the province, particularly in the south-east corner. The north receives rather less snow than the south, even though winter lasts longer. In the agricultural regions, there is an average of 100 frost-free days each year, with the growing season lasting from May to September.

RUPERT'S LAND

In 1610 the English navigator Henry Hudson was searching for a north-west passage to the Orient, braving the ice in his little ship *Discovery*. Entering what is now known as Hudson Bay, he was convinced he was in the Pacific ocean.

Hudson and his crew spent a miserable winter in James Bay. Such ill-feeling developed that in spring there was mutiny. Hudson, his son, the ship's carpenter, and eight men suffering from scurvy were cast adrift. It is not known what became of them, but after a terrible voyage the surviving mutineers reached Ireland.

News of Hudson's voyage excited great interest in England. A second expedition was equipped to look for the missing mariner and at the same time continue his search. In command was Sir Thomas Button, a Welshman, and two of the mutineers were recruited to guide him. In 1612 Button set sail with two ships, one of them the *Discovery*.

Button's expedition wintered at the mouth of a large river which Button named the Nelson, commemorating one of his sailing masters who died there of scurvy. Many other men died too, and Button was forced to abandon one of his vessels, but in spring he sailed north up the coast of Hudson Bay and explored the mouth of the Churchill.

Button did not find a north-west passage, but returned to England convinced that one existed. Within a few years a Danish expedition set out in that hope. Led by Jens Munck, a Norwegian, it wintered at the mouth of the Churchill. Again, most of its members died of scurvy, but Munck and two companions reached home in 1620.

The search for a north-west passage moved to the Arctic, but from 1668 Hudson Bay became a valuable goal in its own right. In that year two adventurers from New France, Pierre-Esprit Radisson and Médard Chouart, Sieur des Groseilliers, arrived in Europe to seek an audience with Charles II. They wanted to open Hudson Bay to the fur trade.

It is not clear whether the Frenchmen themselves had visited Hudson Bay, but they understood its potential. They had earlier approached the French court with their idea, but had been rebuffed. There was a more sympathetic reaction from Charles II's cousin Prince Rupert, who agreed to sponsor a trading expedition to the Bay that the Frenchmen lead.

Radisson sailed in the *Eaglet*, but was forced back by storms. Groseilliers was in the *Nonsuch*, which successfully negotiated Hudson Strait and reached the mouth of the Rupert river on James Bay. There a log fort was constructed, and by summer's end Groseilliers had amassed a rich haul of valuable pelts traded from local Indians.

The *Nonsuch* and its cargo reached England safely, and delighted Prince Rupert and his associates. In 1670 Charles II granted a charter to the 'Governor and Company of Adventurers of England trading into Hudson's Bay,' making them 'true and absolute Lords and Proprietors' of Rupert's Land, the territory drained by rivers emptying into Hudson Bay.

In the course of attacking York Factory in 1697, D'Iberville's ship the *Pelican* was wrecked off the mouth of the Nelson river. In spite of the disaster, the crew salvaged several cannon and laid siege to the fort until the English were forced to capitulate.

The adventurers quickly turned their proprietorship to advantage. By 1685 there were three trading forts at river mouths in James Bay (Rupert's House, Moose, and Albany) and York Factory had been established at the mouth of the Nelson. The sudden English intrusion posed a serious threat to domination of the fur trade by New France.

In 1686 a French expedition travelled overland from Quebec to James Bay. Led by Pierre, Chevalier de Troyes, it included Pierre le Moyne, later Sieur d'Iberville, and his brother, and it quickly overcame the three English posts. York Factory, however, remained in English hands. In 1690 Henry Kelsey, a company apprentice, set off from there to contact Indian tribes in the interior.

Kelsey had been on the Bay since 1677, and had learned the Cree language. He aimed to encourage peace among rival Indian tribes, and so permit bands to carry furs to York Factory without fear of attack on the way or on the journey home. Kelsey spent two winters in the valley of the Saskatchewan, based near the site of The Pas, and he was the first white man to see the prairies.

In 1693 three English ships under Capt. Mike Grimmington wintered at York Factory, and in spring their crews recaptured Fort Albany from the French. There the initiative ended, for in 1694 d'Iberville returned to the Bay after campaigning in New England. Accompanied by a naval force, he landed guns at York Factory and forced its surrender.

Posts had changed hands frequently, and in general the French had the best of things. But at no point did they hold all the posts at once. In 1696 the English recaptured York Factory, only to lose it to d'Iberville the next year. The French victory followed a naval battle in which d'Iberville's *Pelican* took on three English ships and beat them, only to be wrecked itself. The French were able to salvage enough cannon to besiege the fort and force it to capitulate.

The Treaty of Ryswick, signed in 1697, halted the war between England and France, leaving the French with three posts on Hudson Bay and the English with only one, Fort Albany. There was no further fighting, but under the Treaty of Utrecht, signed in 1713, all forts were handed back to the English.

Public Archives of Canada, C-33615

Native Peoples

Europeans could not have developed a fur trade without the help of native peoples. Artifacts brought to light in Manitoba show that the forerunners of today's Indians and Inuit moved into the region 12 000 years ago, when glacial ice was still on the retreat.

Cultures rose and fell, and the stone age was succeeded by the age of iron and pottery. At all times native peoples lived close to the land, hunting, fishing, harvesting wild rice and other plants, using waterways to develop complex trade links with their neighbours.

When the first white men arrived, they encountered Chipewyans and Inuit in the north, and Crees in the woodlands south of Hudson Bay. Saulteaux (or Ojibway) lived in what is now central Manitoba, and Assiniboines (or Stoneys) occupied the west-

Plains Indians like the Assiniboines lived by the buffalo, driving them into 'pounds' where they could be slaughtered. George Beck's drawing shows the technique in use about 1820.

ern plains. More Ojibway were in the deciduous forest of the south-east corner.

In the period of rivalry between French and English, Crees sided with the French, while Chipewyans and Assiniboines supported the English. There was as much hostility between the tribes as they collected furs as there was between their European allies, and Indians played a major part in the conflicts of the later years of the seventeenth century.

Indians of the woods made extensive use of Manitoba's river system. Paul Kane's painting shows the scene at White Mud Portage on the Winnipeg river, about 1850.

National Gallery of Canada

Public Archives of Canada, C-1918

THE FRONTIER

Re-established at York Factory in 1714, the British of the Hudson's Bay Company awaited the arrival of Chipewyan Indians from the west. Few materialized, for most were intercepted and robbed by Crees who had become allies of the French in the south.

In frustration, the factor at York Factory, James Knight, sent his deputy, William Stewart, to arrange peace. In 1715 Stewart met representatives of the Chipewyans, Crees, and other tribes in the forest south of Great Slave Lake.

Peace was made, but two years later the Crees were on the warpath again.

For the sake of the Chipewyans, Knight built a new trading post some way north of York Factory, out of reach of the Crees. He named it Fort Churchill, in honour of the great soldier John Churchill, Duke of Marlborough, a former governor of the Hudson's Bay Company. Within a few years the post burned down, and the British prepared to build a new one.

Traditionally, trading forts consisted of no more than log huts and palisades. At Churchill, however, the Hudson's

York Factory at the mouth of the Nelson river, as painted by Peter Rindisbacher in 1821. The post was the Hudson Bay Company's chief depot on the coast, and remained so until after World War I.

Bay Company decided to build a major stone fortress, to be known as Fort Prince of Wales. Construction began in 1731, and the design called for ramparts 100 m square and 10 to 15 m thick.

The chief justification for the structure was fear of the French, who were quickly expanding their operations in the south and seemed likely to attack their rivals on the Bay. In the year that construction started at Churchill, an expedition of trade and exploration left Montreal for the west. It was led by Pierre Gaultier de Varennes, Sieur de la Vérendrye.

While managing a trading post north of Lake Superior, La Vérendrye had been told of a 'western sea' at the end of a great river. White men lived beside it and they wore armour and rode horses. La Vérendrye believed that the white men were Spanish, the traders living in settlements on the Pacific.

No man had crossed the continent before, and it was not known how wide it was. Louis XIV of France agreed to grant La Vérendrye a trading monopoly west of Lake Superior, expecting him to

A reconstruction of Fort La Reine, originally built by members of the La Vérendrye expedition in 1738, near the site of Portage la Prairie.

subsidize his explorations from profits. So it was that La Vérendrye embarked on his venture.

Setting out with two sons and a nephew, La Vérendrye and his men first travelled to what is now the far west of Ontario. La Vérendrye built a fort on Rainy Lake, which served as his headquarters. The nephew built a fort on Lake of the Woods, and one of the sons built Fort Maurepas near where the Red river empties into Lake Winnipeg.

In 1738 La Vérendrye was in a position to set off for the west. He and two sons crossed Lake Winnipeg, then paddled up the Red river to the present site of Winnipeg at the mouth of the Assiniboine river. There they encountered Crees and built Fort Rouge, which was occupied for only two seasons and then abandoned.

Paddling up the Assiniboine, La Vérendrye and his companions reached the site of Portage la Prairie. There they built Fort La Reine, named in honour of Louis XIV's queen, to trade with local Assiniboines. From there, the adventurers set off towards the south-west, in search of the Spanish.

And so La Vérendrye passed into territory that today belongs to the United States. He never did reach the 'western sea,' but he did push the frontier of exploration far across the continent. Moreover, he sent his son François to develop the fur trade of the north-west.

In 1739 François, Chevalier de la Vérendrye, built Fort Dauphin near Lake Winnipegosis and Fort Bourbon on Cedar Lake. He then ascended the Saskatchewan river, and on another expedition he and his brother Louis-Joseph were the first white men to see the Rocky Mountains from the east. Another brother, Pierre, may have had a hand in building Fort Paskoyac near the site of The Pas in 1750.

The French efforts diverted much of the fur trade previously monopolized by the posts of Hudson Bay, and the British were forced to seek new contacts in the interior. In 1754 Anthony Henday left York Factory with a party of Indians, instructed to persuade other bands to make the long trip to Hudson Bay.

Henday travelled up the Hayes river and then up the Saskatchewan, and went as far west as the Red Deer river in Alberta, where he spent the winter. On the way back he met French traders at The Pas. Soon other Hudson's Bay representatives followed in his footsteps, but within six years Britain's capture of New France spelled the end of French initiatives in the interior.

In spite of the elimination of the French, work proceeded on Fort Prince of Wales. It was not completed until 1771, and even then few men were available to man its defences. Only 40 were present in 1782 when a French force of three ships arrived off the fort, apparently ready to attack.

Commanding the French was the admiral-geographer François de Galaup, Comte de la Pérouse. In charge at the fort was Samuel Hearne, famous as the discoverer of the Coppermine river leading to the Arctic ocean. Hearne knew that the British position was hopeless

A striking statue of Pierre Gaultier de Varennes, Sieur de la Vérendrye. It stands outside Manitoba's Legislative Building in Winnipeg.

and immediately surrendered.

For two days the French laboured to destroy the fortifications, but could make little impression on them. A year later, the British built a modest log fort eight kilometres away, and the stone fortress was abandoned.

Fort Prince of Wales in the mouth of the Churchill was completed in 1771, but abandoned in 1782 after an attack by the French. The fort has been partially restored by Parks Canada.

ASSINIBOIA

The collapse of New France in 1760 left a vacuum in the interior. Trading posts were abandoned, and Indian trappers long loyal to the French turned again to the British of the Hudson's Bay Company. Then English-speaking fur traders from New York moved to Montreal and prepared to compete.

Most of the New York traders were of Scottish background, and for them the Hudson's Bay Company's claims to all Rupert's Land meant nothing. Insisting that they had inherited French rights to the interior, some of the Montrealers ventured there themselves and others employed Canadian woodsmen (*coureurs de bois*) to go on their behalf.

By the 1770s the Hudson's Bay Company was seriously hampered by the 'pedlars,' as it described the Montreal men. The company was being forced to seek out its own trading agreements and to establish posts in the interior. In the 1780s, an even greater threat arose when nine groups of pedlars came together as the North West Company.

In the nineteenth century, Norway House on the Nelson river north of Lake Winnipeg was busier than York Factory. At Norway House convoys bound to and from the interior transshipped furs to a convoy bound for the shore of Hudson Bay, and received trading goods in return. A watercolour by Peter Rindisbacher, 1821.

The new company was a loose grouping of independent firms each holding shares in its operations. They co-operated to build a major field headquarters at Grand Portage, at the western end of Lake Superior. In addition they built trading posts in the interior. One was Fort Gibraltar, near the present site of Winnipeg, and there was another at Souris, near where the Hudson's Bay Company built Fort Brandon.

Nor'Westers like Alexander Mackenzie pushed the trading frontier far to the west, in fact to the Pacific. They and the Hudson's Bay Company competed fiercely for available furs until in 1807 the British concern suffered a devastating blow. When Napoleon organized a continental trade embargo against Britain, the company's European market was cut off.

The Nor'Westers were able to bypass the embargo by dealing through the United States, and their position was immeasurably strengthened. For some time, prominent Nor'Westers had tried to persuade the Hudson's Bay Company to grant them access to the interior through Hudson Bay, but had been refused. Now they set out to buy control of the whole company.

Hudson's Bay stock had plummeted in value, but the company had a champion — Lord Selkirk, a wealthy Scottish philanthropist who had married the heir to a fortune in company stock. Selkirk increased his stake in the company, and

with his brother-in-law Andrew Wedderburn staved off the Nor'Westers' challenge.

One of Selkirk's pet projects was resettlement of impoverished Irish and Scots driven from the estates of landowners. He had already established modest colonies in Prince Edward Island and Upper Canada (Ontario), but his dream was to settle Rupert's Land. His influence as a stockholder procured him an immense grant of land at a nominal fee.

Selkirk's grant covered much of what are now Manitoba, Saskatchewan, North Dakota, and Minnesota. From the company's viewpoint, settlement would reinforce its claims to Rupert's Land and at the same time disrupt the Nor'Westers' supply lines. In 1811 Selkirk sent agents to recruit colonists from the Hebrides, Glasgow, and the west coast of Ireland.

The Nor'Westers did their best to frustrate Selkirk's plans, and no more than 35 settlers sailed with that year's Hudson Bay convoy. They reached York Factory late in the season and were obliged to remain there for the winter. Next summer they travelled up the Hayes river and so to 'Assiniboia,' as Selkirk named his settlement.

The colonists reached their destination on the Red river in late summer. At the suggestion of local Saulteaux Indians and their chief, Peguis, they soon moved south to the neighbourhood of what is

A view of Fort Douglas, first erected by Lord Selkirk's settlers at the confluence of the Red and Assiniboine rivers in 1813. This watercolour is based on a sketch believed to have been made by Selkirk himself during his visit of 1816.

now Pembina, North Dakota, in pursuit of the migrating buffalo herds. There they established Fort Daer and remained for the winter. In spring they returned to the mouth of the Assiniboine and developed 'Colony Gardens' near the Nor'Westers' Fort Gibraltar.

For several years settlers repeated these migrations, each season joined by more colonists sent out from Europe by way of Hudson Bay. Their relations with the neighbouring Nor'Westers were cordial enough, but Métis of the interior — horse-riding frontiersmen who were descended from French *coureurs de bois* and Indian mothers, and manned canoes and hunted buffalo for the Nor'Westers — were less friendly. Métis saw the settlers as a threat to their way of life.

In 1815 Miles Macdonell, Selkirk's agent at Colony Gardens, issued a startling proclamation banning unauthorized export of furs and foodstuffs from Assiniboia. The Nor'Westers' post at Souris was raided, and quantities of dried-meat rations were seized. The local Nor'Westers did not retaliate, but reported the whole matter to their headquarters, which had moved to Fort William on Thunder Bay.

At Fort William it was decided to harass Selkirk's settlers and pressure them into leaving. The next year a series of encounters culminated in the arrest of Macdonell, who was taken east. The settlers were offered safe passage to Upper Canada, and most accepted. Others took refuge at the Hudson's Bay Company post of Norway House.

Only regular Hudson's Bay personnel remained at Fort Douglas, the post built at Colony Gardens. It seemed that Selkirk's colony was doomed. Then in 1816 a large party of new settlers arrived from Hudson Bay and soon afterwards

a party of Canadian voyageurs from Lower Canada, recruited to help defend Assiniboia.

In retaliation for Métis harassment, the voyageurs and some of the new settlers seized the Nor'Westers' Fort Cumberland and later destroyed it, and soon afterwards captured the Nor'Westers' post at Pembina. The onslaught was more than enough to upset the Métis, who joined forces to destroy the settlers once and for all.

The settlers were forewarned of Métis intentions and went out to meet them. At a spot known as Seven Oaks, the Métis surrounded them and a shooting-match ensued. Twenty colonists and one Métis were killed, and many more were wounded. The Nor'Westers took possession of Fort Douglas, and the surviving colonists

were left to seek refuge at remaining Hudson's Bay posts.

Meanwhile, Lord Selkirk himself was in Canada, and had gone to Fort William with a small army of mercenaries to confront directors of the North West Company. Several of them he arrested and sent to Montreal. Then he proceeded to the Red river and recaptured Fort Douglas. His agents persuaded the dispersed settlers to return, and Selkirk laid out a new township for them.

Selkirk was later sued by the Nor'Westers for wrongful arrest, and died a disappointed man. His colony, however, prospered, and in 1821 the threat of the North West Company was eliminated for all time. On the urging of the British government, its directors agreed to amalgamation with the Hudson's Bay Company.

A group of Ojibways meets the governor of the Red river colony in 1825. Peter Rindisbacher's watercolour shows the Saulteaux chief Peguis (standing, in blanket) and the governor (seated, right) in a reception room at Fort Douglas, 1825.

FORT GARRY

In 1821 the Hudson's Bay Company, recently united with the Nor'Westers, built a new trading post at the junction of the Red and the Assiniboine. The post was named Fort Garry to honour Nicholas Garry, who was organizing the amalgamation of the two companies' interests.

For several years the post had a monopoly of trade in and out of the Red river settlement. The only route possible was by way of Hudson Bay. Then independent fur traders established a trading post at St. Paul in Minnesota, about 65 km south of Fort Garry on the banks of the Mississippi.

The Mississippi provided a route to the Gulf of Mexico and so to the world outside, more efficient than the Hudson Bay route because it was open throughout the year. Red river Métis pioneered a new trade route to St. Paul, with goods

Red River carts at Fort Garry in 1875, as painted by Frank Lynn. The cart was the chief mode of transport across the prairies throughout the nineteenth century, in spite of the hideous screech from its ungreased wheels.

loaded on two-wheeled carts each towed by a single ox.

At this time the Red river settlers consisted of the Hudson's Bay men, Métis attached to the fur trade and engaged in hunting buffalo, white homesteaders scattered along the banks of the two rivers, and Roman Catholic and Anglican missionaries. Close by lived bands of Indians, most of them Ojibways.

In charge of the Roman Catholic mission was Father Joseph Provencher, who had come to the Red river in 1818 at Lord Selkirk's request. Selkirk donated land for the mission across the river from what became Fort Garry, and Provencher ministered to Catholics who spoke three languages — English (the Scots and Irish), French (the Métis), and German (disbanded mercenaries who had

After a disastrous flood destroyed the first Fort Garry in 1826, Governor George Simpson decided to build a new fort on higher ground 32 km downstream. Lower Fort Garry was completed in 1832, and survives as a national historic park.

served in Selkirk's private army).

Because the Germans made up the majority of his congregation, Provencher dedicated his church to Germany's apostle, St. Boniface. Within two years, Rev. Benjamin West arrived at the Red river to establish an Anglican mission. He immediately built the settlement's first school, opened in 1820. The first Roman Catholic school was opened in 1823.

The Red river settlers reaped a bumper harvest in 1824, and it looked as if the colony was firmly on its feet. Then in 1826 a devastating spring flood forced the settlers to flee to higher ground. One by one, wooden buildings floated off towards Lake Winnipeg, and by the time the Red river reached its highest level, scarcely a house survived intact.

Fort Garry's buildings and palisades were destroyed with the rest of the settlement. George Simpson, who in 1826 took charge of the Hudson's Bay Company's operations from the eastern coast of Hudson Bay to the Rockies, decided that it should be rebuilt in stone on higher ground 32 km downstream.

Construction of the new post, later known as Lower Fort Garry, began in 1830. Limestone was quarried near by, and stonemasons erected various structures including a governor's residence. Meanwhile, the Red river settlers re-established themselves at the forks upstream, apart from a few who had lost heart and given up.

The disastrous flood of 1826 was not repeated, and settlers gained in confidence. Their trade with St. Paul steadily increased, to the dismay of the Hudson's Bay Company. Simpson responded to the competition by building yet another Fort Garry on the site of the first, this time constructed in stone. It was completed in 1837.

Simpson's move was in vain, for by this time settlers were pouring into Minnesota and the Mississippi was becoming a major trade route. During the 1840s the ox-carts gave way to York boats, and in 1859 an enterprising American transported the parts of a paddle-steamer to the upper reaches of the Red river. Soon assembled and launched, the *Anson Northrup* became the first powered transport to reach Fort Garry.

Public Archives of Canada, C-1059

Buffalo Hunting

Long before white men arrived on the plains of the interior, Indians had hunted the great herds of buffalo that roamed there. The Métis inherited the prowess of their forebears, and each year undertook two major hunts from the Red river.

One hunt set off from Pembina, looking for buffalo in what is now North Dakota. The other travelled west on the Assiniboine to the valley of the Qu'Appelle river. In both cases the hunters were away for weeks, but they returned with rich spoils that represented much of their income for the year.

On the Pembina hunt, as many as 1000 parties travelled in convoy, the hunters on horseback and old men, women, and children in ox-carts. The hunters elected ten captains, and one of these became chief captain and head of the camp. Each captain selected ten 'soldiers' to keep order in his section, and there were also ten guides to locate the buffalo.

The guides took turns to lead the hunt, flying a flag from their carts. The cavalcade rolled across the plains from dawn to dusk, and at night the carts and tents were ranged in a wide circle with draft animals corralled inside. The arrangement protected them from surprise attacks by marauding Sioux.

When buffalo were spotted, control

A buffalo hunters' camp on the prairies. George Seton's watercolour was based on a sketch by William Napier of the Canadian Red River Expedition, the survey party that travelled through what is now Manitoba in 1857 and 1858.

of the hunt passed from the guides to the chief captain. The horsemen ranged themselves in a long line. First they trotted, then galloped towards the buffalo, and rode among them as they stampeded, firing at point-blank range.

If their luck held, the hunters made runs on several successive days. At the end of each run, they located the animals they had killed and left their women and children to recover hides and cut up the carcasses. Hides were scraped and stretched, and delicacies like tongue and hump were often cooked and eaten on the spot. Later, fat was removed, meat was cut in strips for drying, and bones were cracked for their marrow. When ready, most of the dried meat was made into pemmican, pounded into a powder and mixed with hot fat and berries, then poured into pouches to solidify.

The ox-carts carried meat, pemmican, hides, and other products to Fort Garry for sale to the Hudson's Bay Company. The pemmican was issued as rations to the *hommes du nord*, the 'men of the north,' who crewed on York boats and canoes and linked trading posts throughout the northwest.

METIS POWER

In 1867 the Canadas, New Brunswick, and Nova Scotia linked hands in Confederation, and the United States purchased Alaska from Russia. Assiniboia was once more part of Rupert's Land, transferred back to the Hudson's Bay Company by the heirs of Lord Selkirk.

For a time it appeared that the Americans might try to add Rupert's Land to their acquisitions, whether by purchase or annexation. In those circumstances, the new Canadian government led by John A. Macdonald pressured the British into demanding that the Hudson's Bay Company cede its territories to the young Dominion.

Terms were negotiated in 1868 and 1869, and the company agreed to surrender its exclusive rights to Rupert's Land to the Crown. In return the company was to be compensated with a cash settlement amounting to $1.5 million, the sites of its trading posts, and one-twentieth of the land in areas of agricultural settlement.

Canada was scheduled to take over its new 'North West Territories,' among them Assiniboia, in December 1869. The Canadian government prepared to build a road to the Red river from Ontario, passing through Canadian territory, and sent in military surveyors to lay out square townships in readiness for hordes of colonists.

On the Red river the surveyors met problems. Much of the land fronting the river was occupied by Métis, whose farms were long strips stretching inland. Behind the farms was commonage on which all could cut hay. The surveyors proposed to lay out the commonage as farm holdings for new settlers, but the Métis forced them to stop work.

Prominent among the Métis was Louis Riel, a young man of 25 recently returned from a seminary in Montreal. Riel persuaded his people to set up a *Comité National des Métis* (National Council of Métis) which could protest the threats to their traditional way of life. The council's first step was to occupy Fort Garry and dispossess the Hudson's Bay Company.

When news arrived that the Canadians were sending a lieutenant-governor to the North West Territories, the council sent men to intercept him at the United States border and prevent him from crossing. Then they published a 'list of rights' documenting the guarantees Métis wanted from the Dominion government, notably protection of their rights of land, religion, and language, and a say in their own government.

The Métis comprised three-fifths of the population of Assiniboia. Many of the English-speakers were halfbreeds too, descended from Scottish fur traders and their Indian wives, and did little to oppose the Métis. But several dozen loyal Canadians led by Thomas Schultz, an Ontarian, took violent exception to the Métis' initiatives. The Canadians barricaded themselves in a storehouse until flushed out by the Métis, and were then locked up in Fort Garry.

Meanwhile the Hudson's Bay Company had abdicated its responsibility for Rupert's Land, even though the Canadian government was refusing to take over until the Assiniboia 'disturbance' had been quelled. The *Comité National* obligingly filled the vacuum by proclaiming itself the provisional government of Assiniboia, with Riel as president.

Understanding the delicacy of the situation, the Dominion government sent a commissioner, Donald A. Smith, to examine the problem at first hand. Smith, an experienced Hudson's Bay Company trader, twice addressed large meetings of Métis and persuaded them to send delegates to Ottawa to explain their demands.

Smith also prevailed on the Métis to release the Canadians imprisoned in Fort Garry, though a number of them had already escaped. One of them, Thomas Scott, was ejected from Assiniboia and instructed never to return. In spite of this, Scott made his way to Portage la Prairie. There he contacted Ontarian settlers, and persuaded them to march on Fort Garry.

The effort was a fiasco, and those responsible were arrested. Once more locked up in Fort Garry, Scott became violently abusive and was put on trial. Charged with insubordination, he was found guilty and sentenced to death. The next day he was executed by firing squad.

Riel intended the harsh sentence to serve as a warning to other Canadians in Assiniboia. It had repercussions throughout Canada and particularly in Ontario, where Protestant Orangemen recognized Scott as one of their own. When the Métis delegates arrived in Ottawa, two of them were arrested and charged with murder.

The two were soon released, and allowed to present their case to Macdonald. At the last moment Riel had

Métis and other settlers of the Red river colony delighted in the Red river jig, a lively stepdance in which partners tried to outshine each other in the intricacy of their footwork.

instructed them to demand provincial status for Assiniboia, renamed 'Manitoba' so that its boundaries could be much increased. Macdonald was agreeable, and the Dominion parliament prepared to debate what was eventually passed as the Manitoba Act.

For the time, the provisional government of Assiniboia continued to sit, waiting for a Canadian lieutenant-governor to take over. Still worried about American ambitions in the north-west, the Dominion government arranged to send an expeditionary force to the Red river to keep the peace in the new province.

Led by Col. G. J. Wolseley, the force was remarkable for the number of Ontarian volunteers that it contained. Many made no secret of their ambition to take revenge on the Métis for the execution of Scott. Refused permission to travel through American territory, the force made the difficult journey from Lake Superior to the Red river overland.

To the last, Riel was sure that the Canadians would grant an amnesty to Métis involved in the troubles in Assiniboia. As Wolseley's force approached Fort Garry, he was warned of what might happen to him. He escaped

across the river to St. Boniface, and fled to the United States.

In later years, Riel was twice elected to the Dominion parliament to represent a Manitoba riding. He visited Ottawa only once, crossing from Quebec under heavy disguise, because by entering Ontario he risked arrest for murder. As it was, in 1875 he was banished from Canada for five years, and the founder of Manitoba took refuge in the United States.

Louis Riel's *Comité National des Métis*, **which in 1870 proclaimed itself the provisional government of Assiniboia. Riel was president, and here sits in the middle.**

Following the Red river disturbance of 1870, a military expedition was despatched from Canada to restore order. Commanded by Col. G. J. Wolseley, the expedition travelled most of the way by boat, as in this contemporary oil painting by Mrs. F. A. Hopkins.

A settler's homestead near Carberry, painted by E. Roper. Built of logs and roofed with sod, such homesteads usually consisted of a single room with a curtained recess containing the parents' bed.

Manitoba's first Mennonite settlers arrived in 1874. Each year Mennonites gather at Steinbach to celebrate Pioneer Days, when the life of their forebears is remembered in demonstrations of ploughing and other arts.

HOMESTEADS

When Manitoba became a province, three-quarters of its population of 12 000 were French-speaking. Many settlers expected that the proportion would increase. The Manitoba Act recognized French as an official language, and provided for a style of government like Quebec's.

Within a year, the French bias was reversed. The first legislature — a small council appointed by the lieutenant-governor, and an assembly consisting of 12 English-speaking and 12 French-speaking representatives — voted to adopt the laws of Ontario rather than the civil code of Quebec.

The moves foreshadowed massive immigration to Manitoba, not from Quebec as expected, but from Ontario. In response to the urgings of the Dominion government, farm families disillusioned with the stony soils of Ontario's western counties sold up and moved west, where large areas of virgin prairie were available.

Military surveyors had divided Manitoba into townships, each six miles (10 km) square and subdivided into 36 sections. Most Ontarians first bought quarter- or half-sections, expecting to build a homestead of logs or even of sod

with a log frame, and eventually to raise crops and livestock.

Even before 1870, many Ontarian families had settled around Portage la Prairie and Stonewall. With the boom in immigration, most of the newcomers made for the wide plains of southwestern Manitoba. There they were joined by groups of colonists who came directly from the British Isles.

One party of settlers from Ontario had originated in Iceland. Leaving home in 1872 after disagreements with their Danish overlords, they lived in Ontario for three years before moving west with the blessing of the Dominion government. The land they selected was north of Manitoba's original boundary, on the western shore of Lake Winnipeg.

There they established 'New Iceland,' which they ran like a small republic. Its capital was Gimli, named for the home of the gods in Norse mythology. In 1876 another party of Icelanders settled in Hecla, after leaving home when a volcano laid waste their farms. In 1881 'New Iceland' became part of Manitoba when the province's boundaries were extended.

The first significant party of settlers from continental Europe were German-speaking Mennonites from the Ukraine, members of a Protestant religious group

Icelanders settled in the Gimli region in 1875, and around Hecla in 1876. Their descendants celebrate their heritage at an annual festival held in Gimli.

founded in the Netherlands and Germany during the sixteenth century. Threatened with conscription into the Russian army in spite of their age-old objections to military service, they sought refuge in North America.

A small party of Mennonite delegates reconnoitred Manitoba in 1873, and were promised religious freedom, exemption from military service, and the right to keep their language alive in their own schools. The first group of Mennonite settlers arrived in the next year, and were soon established on several sections of land reserved for them in the south around the site of Steinbach.

According to Mennonite custom, the settlers laid out small villages centred on a church and school. Each farmer built a house fronting the village street, and farmed a long strip of land stretching away behind it. In 1876 a second party of Mennonites settled in the area of Winkler and Altona.

In 1884 the Canadian Pacific Railway was completed, and the Dominion government sponsored immigration drives in northern and eastern Europe and the United States. There was enthusiastic support from Scandinavia and the Ukraine. Between 1896 and 1914, more than 30 000 Ukrainians arrived in Manitoba, many with little more than the clothes they were wearing.

Influenced by their church leaders, the Ukrainians aimed to settle in groups. They were not able to obtain sufficient space in the fertile areas of the southwest, so chose land farther north in the parkland belt. It was not so fertile, but they were compensated by plentiful timber supplies.

There the Ukrainians built thatched cottages like those they had left in Europe. Outside the cottages appeared simple, but inside they were decorated with a rich treasure of ornaments recalling Ukrainian civilization. Like the Mennonites, the Ukrainians had much to teach the Ontarians about dry land farming, and their influence is still felt in Manitoba.

The first Ukrainians to arrive were all from the countryside, but they were followed by former city-dwellers who knew nothing of farming. Some of the later arrivals sought work in Winnipeg, like other Europeans arriving soon after the turn of the century. Others went to work for the railways, or for farmers requiring hired help.

Ukrainians, Mennonites, and other Manitobans of European origin were watched closely during World War I in case they showed sympathy with the enemies of the British Empire. In many cases their privileges, particularly of running schools in their own language, were stripped away. However, Mennonites' views on military service were respected, and no effort was made to conscript them.

As a result, in 1918 many Mennonites living in the United States sought sanctuary in Manitoba and were accepted. So were groups of Hutterites, another German-speaking religious community not unlike the Mennonites in history or beliefs. The Hutterites, who shared all property in common, founded the first of more than 60 *bruderhofs* or colonies that exist in Manitoba today.

The Ontarians

Between 1870 and 1890, nearly as many settlers arrived in Manitoba from Ontario as from all other sources put together. The Ontarians set out to recreate the social climate they had left behind them, and in the process came to wield overwhelming political influence in the young province.

In 1890 this influence secured the abolition of the official status of French in Manitoba. Soon afterwards it created a unitary school system in place of the denominational schools that had existed previously. The former strength of the Roman Catholic church was quickly eroded as Protestant ideals came to the fore.

Between 1890 and 1912 there was little further immigration from Ontario, for the province's surplus rural population was absorbed by its cities. Instead, Manitoba opened its doors to tens of thousands of non-Protestant, non-English-speaking immigrants from such areas as the Ukraine and Poland.

In these years Manitoba's Ontarians prospered, and many turned their attention to startling new issues like women's rights. Led by such figures as Cora Hind and Nellie McClung, suffragettes in Winnipeg forced the provincial legislature to take them seriously, and in 1916 Manitoba became Canada's first province to give women the vote.

With the outbreak of World War I, patriotic Ontarians had noted the dangers presented by Manitoba's 'aliens.' Not a few of them were imprisoned, and from 1916 the political rights of Ukrainians, Poles, Germans, and others of European origin were severely curtailed.

The Europeans survived, and in the years following World War I gradually improved their position, until eventually the old Ontarian dominance was swept away.

Tom Creighton's discovery of deposits at Flin Flon in 1914 led to the launching of Manitoba's base metals mining industry. Here Creighton (third from right) points out the site of his discovery to government officials visiting Flin Flon in 1927, before the start of mining operations.

Laying rails in Manitoba's northland, about 1918. The railroad to Churchill was built in stages, first to The Pas (1910), later to Gillam (1918), and ultimately to Churchill (1929).

THE ECONOMY

In 1914 Winnipeg was riding high as the chief distribution and manufacturing centre for all of Canada's west. There was talk of building a railroad to Churchill, so that western grain could be exported by way of Hudson Bay.

The promising situation was reversed almost overnight. In the first place, the opening of the Panama canal in 1914 meant that goods could be transported between Eastern Canada and British Columbia more cheaply by sea than over land. In the second, the outbreak of World War I heralded a serious drop in grain prices that lasted many years.

Many thousands of Manitobans volunteered to fight and sailed to Europe. When the war ended, they returned home to find the province in depression. There was large-scale unemployment in Winnipeg, fed by a steady flow of jobless leaving the countryside in hopes of better fortunes in the city.

That was the background to increasing militancy in Winnipeg's trade unions. Encouraged by the continuing revolution of the masses in Russia, labour leaders urged workers to gain their ends by strike action. In May 1919 building and metal trades workers went on strike when their right to collective bargaining was denied, and appealed to other unions for support.

The result was the Winnipeg General Strike, which lasted just over a month. Winnipeg came to a stop — except that the strikers allowed essential services to continue. Light, water, and police patrols were provided, bread and milk was delivered, and the telegraph and railways were operating. Theatres and movie houses were encouraged to remain open to amuse the idle.

The strike committee was acting as a government, and that was its downfall. Each day the strike became more unpopular, and the labour movement was split down the middle. Eventually its leaders were arrested and released on bail. A public meeting was called but forbidden by order of the mayor.

The meeting took place anyway, and the mayor read the Riot Act. Police sent in by the Dominion government twice rushed the strikers using clubs. On the second occasion they used pistols too, killing one man and fatally wounding another. The strike was broken and Winnipeg went back to work.

Later, more strike leaders were arrested and a number served prison terms. Several went on to distinguished left-wing political careers. Winnipeg remained quiet, but in the countryside there was ferment on the farms. Disgusted with Liberals and Conservatives alike, farmers were preparing to enter politics.

A steam threshing outfit at Portage la Prairie, 1900. Such outfits travelled from farm to farm and were a feature of prairie life until superseded by combine harvesters.

In two elections that followed, the United Farmers of Manitoba had considerable success, and in 1922 they formed a government. Their bow was shot by 1928, but since 1919 the balance of power had moved away from political parties and towards individuals. Between 1928 and 1958 the province was served by a series of coalitions.

The 1920s saw several more impressive innovations in Manitoba. In 1925 grain farmers formed Manitoba Pool Elevators, a co-operative designed to give them more say in the marketing of their crops. The province's first paper mill went into production at Pine Falls on the Winnipeg river, and the first base metals mine was developed at Flin Flon.

The 1930s brought drought, but Manitoba farmers escaped more lightly than their counterparts farther west. Winnipeg, however, was seriously affected by the worldwide depression. Unrest among the unemployed all across Canada encouraged the formation of the left-wing Co-operative Commonwealth Federation (CCF) in 1932.

The CCF, forerunner of the New Democratic Party, was founded by Rev. J. S. Woodsworth, a leader of the Winnipeg General Strike. The movement had an enthusiastic following in Manitoba from the beginning, but not until 1969 did the New Democratic Party unseat the Conservatives and form a government, only to be defeated by the Conservatives in 1977.

Nowhere in Canada has the political seesaw swung higher or faster than in Manitoba in these years. With each change of government, the province's policy on economic matters has been up-ended like an hourglass. New Democrats believe that prosperity flows from the bottom up; Conservatives believe that it flows from the top down.

During its term in office, the NDP spent large sums on construction projects, ran its own manufacturing enterprises, and framed its labour policies to favour workers rather than employers. Its aim was to place more cash in the hands of lower income groups, and to do that it had to tax private enterprise.

The Conservatives, in contrast, encourage private enterprise in order to create more employment and benefit the whole economy. By cutting government services to a minimum, less revenue is needed to pay for them. Freed of the heavy tax load, private enterprise is expected to flourish, and with it the whole province.

The two approaches are not necessarily contradictory, for both work towards the same end. Nor do they have overwhelming impact on primary industries and the manufacturing sector, except in respect of minimum wages and working conditions. Economic policies can do little to prevent the replacement of workers by machines.

Where they do make a difference is in the construction industry, which the NDP has tended to use as a tool to stimulate the rest of the economy, and in the tertiary sector. Under an NDP government, the public service tends to be more important as an employer than when Conservatives are in office.

Angry strikers topple a streetcar at the height of the Winnipeg General Strike of 1919. Police sent to quell the disturbance broke up the riot and the strikers went back to work.

21

CROPS AND LIVESTOCK

The Selkirk settlers of 1812 planned to create farms like those they had left across the Atlantic. They wanted to be self-sufficient, and needed cattle for milk and beef, sheep to provide wool, hogs and poultry, horses, and grain and vegetables.

Hopes that they could domesticate buffalo cows came to nothing, and they acquired a few head of cattle from local trading posts. They bought horses from Indians and they already had some poultry, but sheep brought out in 1813 died in their first year. The grain crop of 1813 was killed by frost, and only vegetables thrived.

Year after year the settlers were hit by disaster. Frost, conflict with Métis, and ultimately successive plagues of grasshoppers in 1818 and 1819 left them with no seed at all. In the winter of 1820, an expedition travelled from the Red river to the Mississippi to buy seed, and never again was the colony without it.

Lord Selkirk had visited the colony in 1816, and had given orders that livestock was to be brought from the United States. In 1819 an American trader, Michael Dousman, was contracted to buy bulls, cows, oxen, mares, and a stallion in the south, and drive them to Assiniboia.

In 1820 Dousman drove a herd from St. Louis to the American border, but missed the settlers and had to remain there for the winter. Only 19 animals survived. The next year he drove a second herd, but it was seized by Sioux raiders. Finally in 1822 he delivered 170 head, which became the basis of Manitoba's beef industry.

Ten years later, servants of the Hudson's Bay Company travelled south to buy sheep. They rode to St. Louis, but no sheep were to be had. They travelled on to Kentucky, and bought about 1300 sheep and lambs. In spring 1833 the party commenced the long journey home, driving the sheep before them.

Mosquitoes, heat, and rattlesnakes

Grain elevators tower over a field of rapeseed at Bowsman in west-central Manitoba, not far from the Saskatchewan boundary.

took their toll of the flock. Worse still was speargrass, which cut the sheep and left open wounds. The Sioux, who had never before seen sheep, allowed them to pass. Even so, only 251 of the original animals reached Fort Garry, but they were enough to found a large flock.

In the coming decades the number of cattle, sheep, and hogs increased. So did the grain harvest, in spite of frost, floods, and periodic returns of the grasshoppers. Even so, the settlers were looking for a variety of wheat that would mature earlier than those they were used to, to save them from the frustration of losing their crops at the last moment.

In 1868 they were introduced to Red Fife, a variety grown with success in the United States. Not only did it mature quickly, but the wheat was harder than conventional varieties and better suited to milling. It was known as Red Fife after David Fife, a farmer of Peterborough, Ontario, who had introduced it from Europe in 1841.

As in the United States, Red Fife thrived in the Red river valley. At first it was consumed only locally. Then in 1876 the Ontario harvest failed, and a Toronto buyer travelled to the Red river hoping to buy 5000 bushels of wheat

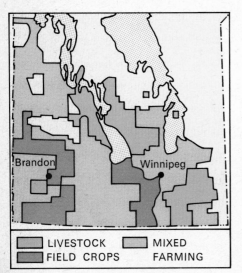

LIVESTOCK   MIXED
FIELD CROPS   FARMING

Mixed farms occupy much of rural Manitoba, but there are large areas in which crops of livestock predominate.

(c.182 m³). Local farmers gleefully co-operated in carrying their grain to a central point for shipment.

Even with this co-operation the grain buyer collected only 587 bushels (c. 21 m³), for no more was available. The shipment travelled south up the Red river by stern-wheeler, then by rail to Duluth, then through Lakes Superior and Huron by lakeboat. Finally it was railed from Sarnia to Toronto, and the way was opened to the great grain trade that made the fortune of Canada's west.

Since 1876, spring wheat has remained the most important crop grown in Manitoba. The coming of the railway, the arrival of new settlers, and the introduction of new grain varieties helped to boost production. Between 1900 and 1914 Manitoba was more prosperous than at any time before or since.

Today, about 35 per cent of the total area in crop production is planted to wheat. About half that area is planted to barley, and lesser proportions to oats, flax, and rapeseed. Many farmers grow specialty crops like sunflowers, sugar beets, mustard, fababeans, potatoes, and field peas.

Specialty crops grow best in the Pembina triangle of the Red river valley, and south of Lake Manitoba. These are the areas with the best soil. Grain is more widespread, extending to the south-east and south-west, and into the region between the big lakes. Vegetables are concentrated in the region of Portage la Prairie.

Cattle thrive in the Dauphin region of the west, and there are large ranches in the south-west. Many of Manitoba's dairy farms are east and north of Winnipeg, within easy travelling distance of the metropolis. Hogs and poultry are raised in specialist operations throughout southern Manitoba.

Flood Control

The rich grass that grew on the plains of Manitoba impeded the flow of the spring run-off, and retained much of the water that inundated the plains during annual floods. Vast areas of the province were little more than swamp.

Early settlers avoided such areas, and later arrivals found that the best land was already occupied. Many built primitive drainage channels to reclaim bogs and marshes, and found that the soil was reasonably fertile. From 1895 land reclamation became a responsibility of the provincial government.

Since then, many millions of hectares of land have been drained. The upkeep of drainage channels is the responsibility of autonomous local water conservation boards, which decide on priorities in their areas. They balance the needs of agriculture, wildlife, and recreation, and pay special attention to the perils of soil erosion.

To protect communities from spring floods, the federal and provincial governments have co-operated in

Flooding in the Red river valley, at St. Norbert. Drainage and dyking systems are being extended to protect its communities from such wasteful inundations.

building dykes. Many kilometres of dykes border the Assiniboine river between Winnipeg and Portage la Prairie. In the Red river valley, communities like Emerson and Morris are surrounded by ring dykes.

Winnipeg is protected by Manitoba's largest flood control project, the Red river floodway, which was completed in 1968. The floodway is a fluid bypass that diverts much of the river's spring flow west of the city where it can do no harm, then delivers it back to the river about 25 km downstream.

A similar floodway has been built on the Assiniboine river upstream of Portage la Prairie. Opened in 1970, the Portage diversion carries water due north to Lake Manitoba. Close to the Saskatchewan boundary at Shellmouth are a dam and reservoir that control the Assiniboine's headwaters and provide a dependable source of water for Brandon and Portage la Prairie.

THE FARMERS

When Winnipeg and Brandon were young, farm families were the rule rather than the exception. Since World War II, however, they have been a declining species. Between 1941 and 1976, the number of farms in Manitoba slumped from nearly 60 000 to few more than 30 000.

Part of the reason for the drop was the abandonment of marginal land that should not have been cleared for farming in the first place. Another part was the amalgamation of small farms to produce efficient units. Between 1941 and 1976, the average size of Manitoban farms rose from about 120 ha to about 250 ha.

In some cases, land is still farmed by the pioneers who cleared it. In others, families benefit from the labours of generations past. Descendants of the original Mennonite settlers still farm in the Steinbach and Winkler-Altona regions south of Winnipeg, and there are still hundreds of Ukrainian families in western Manitoba.

As farms have progressed from being merely self-sufficient to becoming efficient business enterprises, farmers have turned increasingly to machines. In most areas, hired help is a rarity, and the farmer, his wife, and his family attend to all the work that has to be done.

In some cases, neighbouring farmers have found it to their advantage to set up a co-operative, in which they and their neighbours pool their financial resources and expertise. The purpose and scale of such co-operatives vary greatly, but a common factor is that they are run democratically, with each member holding a single vote, regardless of the time and money he has invested.

Some of the co-operatives acquire and develop land. Some are concerned with livestock and dairy operations, as when a group of farmers club together to buy common grazing pasture or develop a feedlot or install milk-producing facilities. Some co-operatives purchase machinery for the use of their members, while some process and market members' products.

The most sophisticated of the small co-operatives are run as colonies by Hutterites, who forswear personal possessions but work hard in managing a rich diversity of farm operations. A typical colony consists of a dozen families on up to 1500 ha of land, raising dairy cows, hogs, and poultry, and growing alfalfa and perhaps wheat.

The most famous of the large co-operatives are Manitoba Pool Elevators and United Grain Growers, which has members throughout Western Canada but has its headquarters in Winnipeg. Both co-operatives were founded by farmers to handle and market grain, but they have expanded to handle livestock and oilseeds also, and to provide their members with farm supplies at reasonable cost.

The many co-operatives, and independent farmers too, have an interest in Manitoba's various marketing boards — producer bodies organized under law to control stages in the marketing of specified commodities. All but two of the eight boards active in the province set production quotas, with the aim of controlling the flow of products to market in order to enhance their price.

The supply of eggs, broiler chickens, turkeys, milk, vegetables, and root crops is affected in this way. The board controlling honey producers sets a minimum retail price, and all hogs must be marketed through the board controlling hog producers. Wheat, oats, and barley for export outside the province must be sold to a national body, the Canadian Wheat Board.

With his grain ready for harvesting, the farmer uses a swather to cut his crop and lay it on the stubble to dry. Later, a combine harvester will gather the swaths and thresh them.

The neat pattern of a Hutterite colony, as seen from the air. Manitoba holds more than 60 such colonies, each of which houses up to 100 members who co-operate in raising crops and livestock and preserving their traditional lifestyle.

FORESTRY

Canada's pioneer forest industries depended on the flow of rivers to carry raw materials to areas where they would be useful. Most of Manitoba's rivers flow north, so for many years the province neglected its own resources and imported timber from Minnesota.

Pine was felled on the headwaters of the Red river, then rafted to Winnipeg, where sawmills cut the wood to shape for use in the frame structures going up all over the city. More wood was floated down the Roseau river, a tributary of the Red river. By the time the Canadian Pacific railway reached Winnipeg, sawmilling was already one of Manitoba's leading industries.

To cross the prairies, the railroad required hundreds of thousands of cross ties for its rails. Cedar and spruce poles cut in south-eastern Manitoba were driven down the Whitemouth river to a mill at Whitemouth. The crosstie industry survived for several decades, serving not only the Canadian Pacific but also its rivals.

The railroads helped forest industries further when they began carrying large logs from eastern Manitoba and western Ontario to the sawmills of Winnipeg. As the railroad system expanded, it provided access to most of the valuable

timber stands of southern Manitoba. In response, several modest sawmills were established on the shores of Lake Winnipeg, notably at the mouths of the Winnipeg and Birkenhead rivers.

In the north, where most of Manitoba's forests lay undisturbed, the Canadian Northern railroad reached The Pas in 1910. Soon a sawmill was established on the Saskatchewan river, and most of its production was railed to Winnipeg. The mill cut both hardwoods and softwoods drawn from the mixed forest fringe that buffers the prairie region from the boreal forest of the north.

Manitoba's first pulp and paper mill was opened at Pine Falls, at the mouth of the Winnipeg river, in the 1920s. Pulpwood for the mill was cut in the surrounding area. The mill was forced to shut down for several years in the 1930s due to lack of demand for paper, but in 1935 it reopened. Since then its capacity has been much increased.

Not until 1972 was a major pulp and paper complex developed at The Pas, together with a modern sawmill. Operated as a provincial Crown agency, Manitoba Forest Resources is organized in three divisions — woodlands operations, sawmills, and pulp and paper production. The best logs harvested are reserved for the sawmills, on the principle that the resulting lumber is consider-

Work in the forests of western Manitoba continues in all seasons. Here a load of logs is collected in winter for transport to the pulpmill at The Pas.

ably more valuable than pulp or paper.

Slabs (facings) from logs processed in the sawmill, as well as logs that are unsuitable for processing as lumber, are converted into chips for pulp and paper production. To make sure that nothing is wasted, sawdust, shavings, and bark from the milling operations are used as fuel to generate steam and electricity for the whole complex.

The method of harvesting most common in both northern and eastern Manitoba is clear-cutting. Loggers remove all trees from forest areas ranging in size from 25 ha to 250 ha, though the average is between 100 ha and 150 ha. Foresters aim to harvest older stands that have reached maturity and that are not utilizing the growth potential of the site. The harvest clears space for new growth.

Trees from the stand are cut and delimbed on the spot, then 'skidded' (dragged) to a central landing. There they are 'bucked' (chopped) into 5 m and 2.5 m lengths and loaded on to trucks, which carry them direct to the mills or to the nearest rail spur.

Trapping

Trapping is Manitoba's oldest industry, and in the north many Métis and Indians and some whites too can still make an adequate living from it. Two programs have ensured the survival not only of the industry, but of a whole way of life.

One of the programs has been the rehabilitation of dried-out Crown marshland, particularly between The Pas and Lake Winnipegosis. Aquatic creatures like beaver and muskrat had been driven from the area, but by controlling the flow of local rivers, water was restored to the marshes and the fur-bearers returned.

The second program, designed to compensate for over-trapping, has been the introduction of registered traplines. Before, trappers worked wherever they liked. With the traplines, each is limited to his own area, and it is in his interest to conserve the fur stocks that it contains.

The institution of the traplines helped to boost production considerably. Far from being endangered, most

of Manitoba's fur-bearing species are in abundant supply. Today, beaver, mink, and muskrat provide about 80 per cent of Manitoba trappers' income, with fox, coyote, and weasel (ermine) accounting for most of the remainder.

Today's trappers rely on snowmobiles rather than dog-teams, but their traditional skills are recalled during the annual Trappers' Festival at The Pas. The festival features the world championship dog derby, in which competitors travel some 220 km over three days.

A typical logging crew consists of a chain saw operator and a skidder operator, but to an increasing extent machines are taking over. Mechanical fellers cut, delimb, and bunch logs in piles of eight or ten. At landings, automatic slashers are taking the place of chain saw operators in bucking logs for the mill.

A provincial forest nursery at Pineland, by the Whitemouth river east of Winnipeg, grows coniferous seedlings to be replanted in cut-over forest land. In addition it grows both deciduous and coniferous seedlings for replanting in Crown land, intended to improve wildlife habitat and check soil erosion.

In the province as a whole, about 60 per cent of the annual cut is pulpwood (chiefly softwood) and about 30 per cent is lumber (softwood or hardwood). The remaining 10 per cent is harvested to make fence posts and mining timbers, or to provide fuel.

The kraft paper mill at The Pas, part of a major forest industry that draws on timber resources from across northern Manitoba.

FISHING

The great lakes of Manitoba hold a richer variety of freshwater fish than any other part of North America. More than 80 species have been recorded, though only 15 of them are harvested commercially.

Some of the species are of the cold water type, for instance lake trout and tullibee. Many more — for instance, whitefish, pickerel, sauger (or perch), bass, and pike — are associated with warmer temperatures. Coldwater species are found in deep lakes and in the far north, with middle temperature species everywhere else.

Today, whitefish are the most common commercial species in the lakes of Manitoba, followed by blue and yellow pickerel (or walleye). The two species make up about 75 per cent of the commercial catch, followed in importance by sauger, pike, trout, sturgeon, and tullibee.

There are three main fishing regions in Manitoba. Lake Winnipeg (fished chiefly by Indians, Métis, and whites of Icelandic descent) provides about 35 per cent of the total catch. Another one-quarter comes from Lake Manitoba (provided, in part, by Franco-Manitobans) and Lake Winnipegosis (where Ukrainians are prominent). The remainder of the catch is drawn from the numerous lakes of the north.

Fish are caught both winter and summer, but the summer catch is larger. For some species, notably mullet, fishermen set stationary trapnets, and for larger species like sturgeon, they must employ baited handlines. Otherwise, most fishermen rely on gillnets, buoyed on the surface and weighted at the bottom to hang vertically in the water and catch fish by their gills.

In summer, several sizes of fishing vessels are used on Lake Winnipeg, the busiest fishery. The biggest are whitefish tugs, between 12 and 14 m long and decked astern, though their bows are open. A mechanical lifter pulls the heavy net from the water. The tugs have crews of two or three men. Yawls, about seven metres long and open, are crewed by two men. Otherwise, individual

A fisherman using a gillnet on Lake Winnipeg. The net is buoyed on the surface and weighted on the bottom to hang vertically in the water and catch fish by the gills.

At a reservation on Lake Winnipegosis, Indian fishermen gut and clean their catch, which will be sold through the Freshwater Fish Marketing Corporation in Winnipeg.

Fishermen return from a day's work on Lake Winnipeg, which produces about 35 per cent of Manitoba's catch. There and elsewhere, whitefish and walleye (pickerel) comprise about 75 per cent of the commercial catch.

fishermen operate in powered skiffs, lifting their nets by hand. This is the method commonly employed on the lakes of the north.

In winter, fishermen resort to large snow tractors or to snowmobiles. When the ice is strong enough, they travel out to select spots to drill holes. Then they thread gillnets under the ice by means of a 'prairie jigger,' an ingenious device invented in Manitoba in the late 1800s.

Fitted with a sprung lever attached to a rope, the jigger is a cedar plank about two metres long. The fisherman lowers the jigger through his hole into the water, where it floats and presses tightly against the underside of the ice. By tugging on the rope, the fisherman pulls the lever and the jigger skates forward.

The fisherman follows the jigger's progress by the noise it makes, and when it has travelled far enough he cuts a second hole in the ice and retrieves it. Next, he attaches a gillnet to the rope, pulls it through the first hole and towards the second, and leaves it weighted in the water until he is ready to retrieve it.

In summer, the catch is iced to keep it fresh. In winter, it is covered in snow to prevent it from freezing. Fresh fish bring higher prices than frozen products, and require minimal processing. Frozen products are processed at plants in Winnipeg, The Pas, Leaf Rapids, and Island Lake.

Since 1969, all freshwater fish caught in the prairie provinces, the Northwest Territories, and north-western Ontario have been marketed by the Freshwater Fish Marketing Corporation, a federal Crown agency with headquarters in Winnipeg. Most of Manitoba's production is destined for markets in the United States.

Besides the thousands of lakes that support the commercial fishery, Manitoba has countless glacial potholes too small to support a permanent fish population. Since the 1960s these have been used to raise rainbow trout, obtained as fingerlings from commercial fish hatcheries and released in the potholes to put on weight.

As many as 200 Manitoba farmers raise rainbow trout as a hobby, largely for their own use. About 30 of them raise trout commercially. In all cases the grown trout are caught by gillnet or by hook and line, either before ice forms or after it has formed, but before the pothole's oxygen supply is exhausted.

In the past there was a significant commercial fishery for beluga whales in Hudson Bay, particularly off Churchill. The fishery was banned in 1967, but a small number of belugas are live-trapped by local fishermen contracted by zoos, aquariums, and research institutions. The belugas are driven into shallow water, secured on inflatable rafts, and carried ashore by stretcher.

Winter fishermen recover a gillnet set by means of a prairie jigger. Beside them is a snow tractor, standard equipment during Manitoba's long freeze.

MINING

In 1911 modest deposits of gold were found at Rice Lake in northern Manitoba. Prospectors flocked to the area, among them a group that included Tom Creighton. In January 1915 Creighton went moose-hunting near the Manitoba-Saskatchewan boundary.

Crossing a frozen lake, Creighton fell through the ice and was soaked to the skin. Lighting a fire to dry his clothes, he noticed highly mineralized ore and believed it was gold. Soon afterwards he and another prospector visited the spot to confirm the find, and later in the year they staked claims.

The lake straddling the provincial boundary had no name, and to register their claims the prospectors had to devise one. Creighton remembered reading a novel in which the hero, one Josiah Flintabbatey Flonatin, investigated a bottomless lake by submarine and discovered a golden city. The prospectors named the lake Flin Flon in Josiah's honour.

Flin Flon's gold was soon worked out, but years later a company was formed to develop extensive deposits of copper and zinc. A rail spur had to be built to link Flin Flon with The Pas, and the lake had to be emptied of water and mud before mining could proceed. Operations started in 1927, at first on the surface but later underground.

To accommodate Flin Flon's miners, houses were built on solid rock, which meant that pipes had to be laid on the surface. Major technical facilities, including a concentrator, zinc recovery plant, and copper smelter, were installed. In one swoop, the wilderness of northern Manitoba was made to serve man's purposes.

The mining firm responsible for developing Flin Flon was the Hudson Bay Mining and Smelting Company (not related to the Hudson's Bay Company). A year after Flin Flon went into production, a copper-zinc mine began operating at Sherridon, about 50 km to the north-east. Sherridon was the first venture of Sherritt Gordon Mines.

Sherridon's ore body was much smaller than Flin Flon's, and during the 1930s Sherritt Gordon hired Austin McVeigh, a well-known prospector, to search the wilds for new deposits. In 1941 McVeigh located an outcrop containing nickel and copper at Lynn Lake, about 200 km to the north.

Until that time, Canada's production of nickel had been monopolized by the two giants of Sudbury in northern Ontario, International Nickel and Falconbridge. The discovery at Lynn Lake was of major strategic importance, quite apart from its economic value, and was kept secret until 1945. Meanwhile, Sherritt Gordon prepared to take advantage of their find by moving the whole community of Sherridon to Lynn Lake.

The move was best made in winter, over snow-covered trails and frozen lakes. Convoys of tractors and sleighs travelled day and night, carrying whole buildings and all the equipment needed for the mine and concentrating plant. The transfer was completed in 1953,

Nickel is mined and refined at Thompson for export worldwide. Here, molten nickel from an oxidizing converter is poured into a ladle before being cast.

Deep underground at Flin Flon, miners drill deep holes for explosives. Their drills are driven by compressed air.

and in the same year the first nickel concentrate was railed to Sherritt Gordon's new nickel refinery at Fort Saskatchewan, Alberta.

Sherritt Gordon's discovery of nickel triggered a major prospecting boom in northern Manitoba, carried out in the air rather than on the surface. Both International Nickel and Falconbridge made aerial surveys of vast stretches of the Precambrian Shield in search of anomalies below that might indicate ore deposits.

International Nickel (or Inco) located the large nickel-copper deposit now mined at Thompson. Rather than wait for a railroad spur to be completed, the company decided to establish a new town, as Sherritt Gordon had established Lynn Lake. Tractors and sleighs hauled lumber, cement, fuel oil, and other supplies to the new mine.

Commercial nickel production at Thompson (named after John F. Thompson, a former Inco chairman) began in 1961. In quantity the production is dwarfed by Sudbury's, but it is the second most significant source of nickel in Canada. The nickel ore is concentrated, smelted, and refined on the spot, and Thompson products are shipped direct to customers all over the world.

In 1969 Inco opened the Birchtree mine near Thompson, and in the same year Falconbridge entered Manitoba with a nickel-copper mine at Manibridge, near Wabowden. Hudson Bay Mining had already opened three new copper-zinc mines at Snow Lake, and it has since opened more mines in that area as well as more at Flin Flon.

All of these base metals producers are exploiting the resources of the Precambrian Shield. Nickel is the most valuable mineral produced in Manitoba, with copper second and zinc third. Industrial minerals, including limestone, quartz, gypsum, and peat moss, are recovered in southern Manitoba, and crude petroleum comes from wells around Virden in the south-west.

Headgears and other surface workings at the base metals mines of Flin Flon, as seen from the top of the smelting stack. Flin Flon's open pit was worked out decades ago, and now the minerals come from underground workings.

Most of Manitoba's metal manufacturing plants are located in Winnipeg, but there is a bicycle factory in Rivers. Here an operator fixes spokes in a wheel.

MANUFACTURING

In 1898 two small plants were established in Winnipeg to make work clothes for the expanding population. Between 1900 and 1925, Winnipeg blossomed as the leading manufacturer of work clothes in Western Canada, and Manitoba's industrial future was assured.

Several factors were responsible. Winnipeg was the leading city of the west, and attracted unskilled labour that was both plentiful and cheap. More significantly, after World War I quantities of warehouse space became available in Winnipeg because the opening of the Panama canal meant that fewer goods were passing through the city. New garment manufacturers moved in and set up shop.

After 1925 the manufacturers began producing low-priced fashion goods as well as work clothes. During World War II the federal government placed huge contracts for uniforms, and another line was added. By 1960 the industry was producing better-quality merchandise for higher-income customers.

The rise of Manitoba's garment industry marked a significant transition. Far from being tied to processing local raw materials as might be expected, Manitoba was adding value to raw materials obtained outside the region. From catering only to the prairie population, Winnipeg manufacturers and those in smaller centres sold goods in other parts of Canada, and ultimately exported them worldwide as is the case today.

Steel is milled in Selkirk, Virden oil is refined near Winnipeg, chemical fertilizers are made in Brandon, plastics products are made in Dauphin. Railroad rolling stock is built in Winnipeg, and communications cables are produced in Portage la Prairie. The only major industries not represented in the province are automobile manufacturing and tobacco processing.

A good example of Manitoba's versatility is base metals production. At Thompson, nickel-bearing ore is mined, concentrated, smelted, and refined, then exported from the port of Churchill. Copper and zinc are smelted at Flin Flon, then forwarded to Montreal for refining.

A glove factory in Winnipeg. Manitoba's garment industry has been a significant force in the economy since 1914.

The Royal Canadian Mint, one of Winnipeg's most impressive buildings, was opened in 1976. The mint strikes copper and nickel coins for Canada and for other countries.

Both nickel and copper are used as raw materials at the Royal Canadian Mint in Winnipeg, opened in 1976. Presses produce coin blanks from strips of metal, and later in the process coining machines mint obverse and reverse designs on hundreds of thousands of coins each day.

Many other metal industries are active in Manitoba, making machinery, transportation equipment, electrical products, and other goods. Telephone components are made in Morden, farm machinery and steel buildings in Brandon, tractors, combine harvesters, and electric trolley buses in Winnipeg, and bicycles in Rivers.

Winnipeg is one of the largest metal manufacturing centres in Canada, but among the many operations concerned, pride of place goes to those in the aerospace industry. In the past whole aircraft were assembled in the province, but today plants concentrate on manufacturing components for jet engines and other parts of aircraft and rockets, and for industries using related technologies.

Forest products are made into newsprint at Pine Falls on the Winnipeg river, and into kraft packaging paper at The Pas. Newsprint contains a high proportion of groundwood pulp produced through friction, while kraft is made from pulp pressure-cooked in chemicals. In both cases the pulp is spread on moving screens, where the freed fibres jell and make paper.

Food and beverages processing comprises the largest single branch of manufacturing in Manitoba, both in value of shipments and employment. Manitoba processors handle animal products, vegetable products, cereals and oils, sugar beets, fish products, beverages, baked goods, and confectionery. Most of the plants are in Winnipeg.

In the past, whole aircraft were built in Manitoba, but today the aerospace industry is specialized. This is a Winnipeg plant that builds aero engines.

Construction

Manitoba has seen three major construction booms during the twentieth century. The first was confined to Winnipeg, between 1900 and 1913. The second followed World War II, when Winnipeg and Brandon caught up on the backlog of construction needs that had accumulated during the 1920s and the 1930s.

The third construction boom began in the 1960s and has continued into the 1970s. It has changed the face of the province, and Winnipeg most of all. Highrise apartment blocks, business premises, and public buildings have lifted the city's skyline high above its surroundings.

Outside Winnipeg, new highways and great hydroelectric dams have opened the door to the resources of Manitoba's north. Major industrial ventures have given birth to Thompson, and added new life to Portage la Prairie, Brandon, and The Pas. Each of the larger communities has grown with new businesses and new housing projects.

WATER POWER

In the eighteenth and nineteenth centuries, Manitoba's great rivers were the lifelines of the fur trade. In the twentieth century, they have been harnessed to generate hydroelectricity, one of Manitoba's most valuable renewable resources.

As early as 1906, a modest generating station was built at Pinawa on the Winnipeg river. Six more stations were developed on the river in later years, the last of them in 1955. The six are still in operation, four belonging to Manitoba Hydro, the provincial utility, and two to Winnipeg Hydro, which services the city's inner core. Together the six stations have a total year-round generating capacity of 560 000 kW.

The Winnipeg river's potential is being exploited to the full, and since 1960 further hydroelectric expansion has been in the north. Even before Manitoba Hydro entered the area, Sherritt Gordon Mines built two private generating stations on the Laurie river. They have since been transferred to the province.

Flin Flon utilized power generated at Island Lake in Saskatchewan, and there was a small local thermal station at The Pas burning diesel fuel. But when International Nickel decided to develop the nickel resources discovered at Mystery Lake, Manitoba Hydro prepared to build a generating station on the Nelson river. The Kelsey station was commissioned in 1960, and has since been enlarged several times to keep pace with expansion in the mines.

With Kelsey complete, Manitoba

Pine Falls generating station on the Winnipeg river, one of several that provide power for the City of Winnipeg.

Hydro turned to Grand Rapids in central Manitoba. A generating station was built to catch the whole flow of the Saskatchewan river where it enters Lake Winnipeg. Commissioned in 1968, the plant has consistently performed better than expected, and its total generating capacity is 472 000 kW.

In 1966 Manitoba Hydro announced the start of a project that would dwarf the schemes undertaken previously. For half a century, power planners had been aware of the potential of the Nelson and Churchill river systems leading to Hud-

Kettle generating station on the Nelson river was built to serve the mines of Thompson, and is now connected to Manitoba's electricity grid.

son Bay. Now Manitoba was ready to make use of them.

As a first step, construction began on a new generating station at Kettle Rapids on the lower Nelson. The river was diverted as a dam and generating facilities were installed, and initial generation began in 1970. Meanwhile, the federal government erected a system of extra-high-voltage transmission lines to carry Nelson power to Winnipeg.

Another element of the scheme was to divert the flow of the Churchill river into the Nelson system by way of the Rat and Burntwood rivers. The extra power would justify the development of new generating stations on the lower Nelson. The diversion scheme was completed in 1976.

At the same time, hydro engineers set out to regulate the flow of Lake Winnipeg, the Nelson's source. Lake Winnipeg's natural outflow is much smaller in winter than in summer, due to ice barriers in the channels leading to Cross Lake downstream. By building three diversion channels and a control dam that also served as a generating station (Jenpeg), the winter outflow could be increased.

The regulatory scheme was completed in 1977, and Jenpeg (total capacity 168 000 kW) produced its first power. Meanwhile, in 1975 Kettle Rapids had reached its maximum output of 1 272 000 kW, and Long Spruce, a new station 20 km downstream of Kettle Rapids, produced its first power in 1977. When completed, it would have a generating capacity of 980 000 kW.

Several more generating stations are slated for the lower Nelson river, but for the time there is no need to develop them. In future it may be possible to exploit the upper Nelson and Burntwood rivers too.

All told, upwards of 8 000 000 kW of power are available from the Nelson-Churchill system — far more than Manitoba will need for its own use. Already a considerable surplus of power is exported to Saskatchewan, Ontario, Minnesota, and North Dakota, and the amount will be increased.

Massive generators are installed at the Jenpeg hydro generating station, on the Nelson river about 45 km north of Lake Winnipeg.

Manitoba's hydroelectric power is cheap and consistent, but the generating system cannot quickly adjust to sudden rises in demand, especially during winter. To cope with emergency peaks, Manitoba Hydro operates coal-burning generating stations at Selkirk (132 000 kW) and Brandon (237 000 kW). On a local basis, small diesel generating stations serve communities not connected to the provincial power grid.

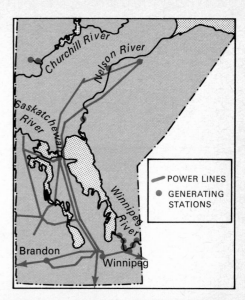

Hydro power is one of Manitoba's most valued resources, and the Nelson and other rivers have been harnessed to produce a surplus for export to neighbouring provinces and the United States.

Winnipeg's international airport, a cross-roads of the air serving Canada north, east, and west, the United States, and Europe by way of the Arctic.

A cloverleaf intersection straddles the Trans-Canada Highway close to the Red river outside Winnipeg. Modern highways are designed to be wide, flat, and as straight as possible, in the interests of safety.

TRANSPORTATION

The opening of Western Canada depended heavily on two modes of transport devised in Manitoba. One was the York boat used in the fur trade, the other the Red river cart invented by Métis and later adopted by migrating settlers.

The York boat took its name from York Factory, where it was introduced about 1800. Before, the fur trade had relied on birchbark canoes of Indian design. As traffic increased, there was a need for larger, sturdier craft that could stand considerable punishment and be handled by a smaller crew.

The vessel that evolved was heavy and cumbersome, about 12 m long and 3 m wide, with a flat bottom that meant it could be rolled over portages. It carried a mast and a square sail, which was handy when the wind was from behind. Otherwise it was poled along the bottom if the water was shallow enough, or rowed if it was not. In rapids it might be 'tracked' — hauled with ropes by men preceding it on the bank.

The Red river cart was invented as a vehicle to carry supplies on buffalo hunts. Constructed of wood and raw-hide available locally, the cart was simply a platform mounted on a pair of wheels, hauled by an ox or perhaps by a pony or horse. Each cart could carry as much as 360 kg in a load.

The advantage of the cart's simple construction was that it could travel where more complex vehicles would have been shaken to pieces. The ox could be led across open country by a rawhide thong attached to its horns. Often as many as six carts travelled as a 'brigade,' one behind the other and with a single driver in charge.

Both the cart and the York boat had long careers, but their importance was eclipsed when a paddle-steamer route was opened on the Red river, with connections to St. Paul and the Mississippi. The first steamer went into service in 1859, and in 1876 the first shipment of wheat from Western Canada was exported by this route.

Two years later Winnipeg and St.

Each year Métis and Indians celebrate York Boat Days at Norway House north of Lake Winnipeg. Until World War I, York boats were in regular use carrying cargoes between Norway House and York Factory, as in the early days of the fur trade.

Paul were linked by railroad. Where before nearly all goods had reached Manitoba by way of Hudson Bay, now they were brought in from the south. With the arrival of the Canadian Pacific Railway in 1885, they came in from the east as well, and with them large numbers of settlers.

In the course of three decades, Winnipeg became the crossroads of Canada. The Canadian Pacific transcontinental system was completed in 1885, and early in the twentieth century two more transcontinental railroads were developed, both passing through Winnipeg. In 1923 they were amalgamated as the Canadian National Railways.

For decades the railroads dominated Canada's transportation network, but since World War II they have been rivalled by highways and air transportation. The Trans-Canada Highway passes through Winnipeg and close to Portage la Prairie and Brandon. Sited so close to Canada's centre, Winnipeg is the natural choice as the transferral point for goods trucked between east and west and vice versa, as well as for goods brought in from the United States.

Fourteen major trucking concerns carry goods between Eastern and Western Canada, and eight of them have their headquarters in Winnipeg. Many eastern and United States carriers truck their goods to Winnipeg, then 'interline' with Winnipeg carriers that carry them to the west.

Southern Manitoba is connected with the north by provincial trunk highways leading to The Pas, Flin Flon, and Thompson, and by railroad to Churchill by way of The Pas and Thompson. In addition, Transair, the prairie regional carrier, provides scheduled flights to all the larger communities in the north.

Transair is based in Winnipeg, which is as much a crossroads of the skies as of highways and railroads. The transcontinental routes of Air Canada and CP Air pass through Winnipeg, and it is served by United States carriers, too. In addition, Air Canada provides direct flights form Winnipeg to Europe over the North Pole.

For three months of the year, Manitoba is connected to the outside world by sea. Churchill has been an ocean port since early in the eighteenth century, but today it handles exports of wheat and nickel rather than furs. Besides serving the interior, Churchill handles cargoes of supplies destined for communities of the western Arctic, which are carried to them by barge.

Churchill's grain terminal dominates the skyline of Manitoba's outlet to the sea. The port is used during no more than three months of the year, because only then can ships navigate the Hudson Strait, the passage to and from the Atlantic around northern Quebec.

Yards and Workshops

Both CP Rail and Canadian National operate major train-marshalling yards in Winnipeg. The CP Rail terminal is one of the world's largest privately owned yards, and CN's Symington yard in St. Boniface is even more extensive.

The central feature of each yard is a man-made hill, or 'hump.' Individual freight cars are pushed over the top and travel down under their own momentum. Controllers switch them to an intricate series of classification tracks, where blocks of cars heading for particular destinations are assembled.

The two yards handle thousands of freight cars each day, destined for points east, west, north, or south. Operations continue around the clock, throughout the year. Both railroads control humping and classifying operations by push-button control, and

The CP Rail terminal in Winnipeg, one of the world's largest privately owned yards. Like its Canadian National counterpart, the yard handles thousands of freight cars every day.

monitor the progress of freight cars with computerized scanners.

Attached to the yards are railroad shops which repair and service locomotives and passenger and freight cars. CP Rail's Weston shops are one of the railroad's three main repair complexes, and they manufacture car wheels for the entire CP Rail system. Canadian National carries out locomotive overhauls and major repairs at its Transcona shops, which constitute the largest industrial plant in the Winnipeg area.

At Gimli on Lake Winnipeg, CN maintains its national training centre. Locomotive engineers, dispatchers, transportation supervisors, and master mechanics are assigned to the school from all parts of Canada.

RAILROADS

There are three main elements in Manitoba's railroad network. The rival tracks of the CP Rail and Canadian National systems intertwine in the south, and in the north Canadian National operates a line to Churchill on Hudson Bay.

Railroads had their start in Manitoba in 1877. Joseph Whitehead, a Winnipeg contractor engaged in laying track to link Winnipeg with Pembina, imported a locomotive, several flat cars, and a caboose from the United States. The little train, the first to be seen on Canada's prairies, reached Winnipeg by river barge.

Whitehead's track was intended to serve as part of the transcontinental 'Canadian Pacific Railway' promised by the Dominion government. The locomotive was optimistically numbered 'C.P.R. No. 1,' and also named *'Countess of Dufferin'* in honour of the wife of Canada's governor-general. Unfortunately it arrived just too late for the ceremony of driving the 'CPR's' first spikes.

Both the governor-general and Lady Dufferin took part in the ceremony. Ironically, Whitehead's Canadian Pacific headed not east or west, but south towards St. Paul. Nevertheless, it was a start, and within a few years the Pembina lines became part of the 'real' CPR incorporated in 1881.

On New Year's Eve 1881, Cornelius

The CP Rail and Canadian National systems cross southern Manitoba, and a northern line stretches to Churchill on Hudson Bay.

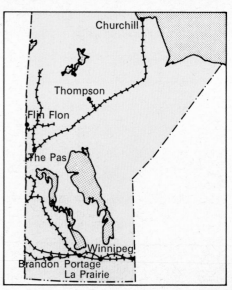

Van Horne, the American engineer appointed general manager of the CPR, arrived in Winnipeg to set up his construction headquarters. As months passed construction crews drove the railroad towards the west. By the end of 1882, Winnipeg was connected by rail with Medicine Hat in what is now Alberta.

In the other direction, Winnipeg was linked with Fort William on Thunder Bay, Lake Superior. The former field headquarters of the Nor'Westers gained new importance as the principal shipping outlet for Western Canada's wheat. Canadian Pacific's trans-continental line was completed in 1885, and trains travelled from coast to coast.

For ten years the CPR enjoyed a monopoly of western rail traffic, to the dismay of Manitoba farmers, who suspected that freight rates were higher than they should have been. Many of them were delighted when two local promoters, William Mackenzie and Donald Mann, prepared to build a rival railway between Winnipeg and Port Arthur on Thunder Bay.

Eventually known as the Canadian Northern Railway, the new line was soon extended west by a route some distance north of Canadian Pacific's. The two railroads competed for available freight and for the attentions of settlers moving into the area. They prospered so handsomely that the Grand Trunk Railway, Eastern Canada's principal carrier, looked for a way to enter the west and share the bonanza.

The Dominion government allowed Grand Trunk to build a new line from Winnipeg west, but itself built the connecting track from Winnipeg east, intending to lease it to Grand Trunk. Construction of both sections of the line began in 1906, but by the time the eastern section was completed, Grand Trunk was no longer interested. The line was operated as Canadian Government Railways (CGR).

World War I left all Canada's railroads short of money. Two of the trans-continental systems, Canadian Northern and CGR-Grand Trunk Pacific, were seriously hit. As a result, by 1923 all lines in Canada, apart from Canadian

Pacific and American railroads operating in Canada, were amalgamated as Canadian National Railways, under the aegis of the government.

The railroad to Churchill was built in stages. Between 1906 and 1910, Canadian Northern built a line from Hudson Bay, Saskatchewan, to The Pas. Between 1911 and 1918 the Canadian government extended the line to Gillam on the Nelson river. In 1928 and 1929 the government built the final section across muskeg and provided Manitoba with a new outlet to the sea.

Today, the rail service between Winnipeg and Churchill is one of Manitoba's leading tourist attractions. Enticed by hopes of seeing Fort Prince of Wales, beluga whales in the river mouth, wild flowers, and even polar bears, visitors from many countries travel in style to explore the treasures of the north.

Winnipeg's railroad enthusiasts preserve the traditions of steam power with the Prairie Dog Central, a special service that carries passengers from Winnipeg to Grosse Isle and back on Sundays and holidays throughout summer.

TOWNS AND CITIES

For a few months in 1867, Portage la Prairie was the capital of a vast 'republic' stretching to the Rocky Mountains. Its president was Thomas Spence, a Scottish storekeeper who had arrived in Assiniboia in the previous year.

Spence was soon disenchanted with the rule of the Hudson's Bay Company, and persuaded rural settlers to petition for a representative council. When nothing happened, he and several others in Portage la Prairie declared their independence.

Naming their republic 'New Caledonia,' they set its boundaries as the 49th parallel in the south, the Rockies in the west, the Arctic in the north, and a line just short of Fort Garry in the east. As president, Spence appointed citizens of Portage la Prairie as his ministers and also as constables.

The constables' chief responsibility was to collect customs duties on goods entering and leaving the republic. This they did with some success until Spence sent two of them to arrest a shoe-

maker for non-payment of taxes. The shoemaker was accused of high treason against the republic.

The trial was attended by farmers of the plains who objected to paying taxes to a non-existent republic. There were interruptions, and Spence ordered more arrests. A scuffle ensued and shots were fired. That was the end of the republic, and Portage la Prairie retreated from the stage of world events.

Portage la Prairie is set on the Assiniboine river east of Brandon, Manitoba's second city. In many respects the communities are twins. Both were founded as fur-trading posts, and both owe much of their importance to the Canadian Pacific Railway.

In the case of Portage la Prairie, the trading post was Fort La Reine, one of those established by the La Vérendryes. The 'portage' was between the Assiniboine and Lake Manitoba, 12 km away. Today, Portage is best known as the hub of an important agricultural region, famous for its vegetables.

Brandon was named after the Duke of Brandon, a director of the Hudson's Bay Company. A trading post, Brandon

Thompson, in northern Manitoba, exists to accommodate nickel miners and their families, but it is not a company town. City planners have created a model community in the heart of the boreal forest.

House, was built close to the site of the present city in 1793, and was several times relocated. The Canadian Pacific selected the site of Brandon station in 1881, and a town grew up around it.

Today, both Brandon and Portage la Prairie are distribution and manufacturing centres. Brandon serves not only western Manitoba but also eastern Saskatchewan. Both communities are on the main line of CP Rail and also on the Trans-Canada Highway, closely linked as they have been since the eighteenth century.

The two cities are balanced by another set of twins in the north, the communities of Thompson and Flin Flon. Both rely heavily on the mining enterprises that are their reason for being, but neither of them are company towns. Both have first-rate educational and recreational facilities to compensate residents for being far from other centres of civilization.

Thompson, Flin Flon, Brandon, Portage la Prairie, and Winnipeg are the five cities of Manitoba. The chief towns are Selkirk, Dauphin, and The Pas. All three of these were founded as fur-trading forts, but have since developed as distribution centres serving the communities that surround them.

Dauphin, named for the heir to the French throne, was established by the La Vérendryes in 1741. Between 1896 and 1898 it was the centre of one of the first areas of Manitoba settled by Ukrainians. The Pas also dates from the age of the La Vérendryes, and is still an important centre of Canada's fur trade and forest industries.

Selkirk was first occupied by independent fur traders about 1767. A century later, it was chosen as the point where the Canadian Pacific railroad would cross the Red river. Then quicksands were discovered, and it was decided that the railroad would cross at Winnipeg.

For a brief period it seemed as if Selkirk would become Manitoba's premier community, but that was not to be. Even so, a significant steel industry has developed in the town, and it is the point where most of the fish caught in Lake Winnipeg are transshipped on their way to the major fish processing plant in Winnipeg.

Brandon, on the Assiniboine river, is Manitoba's second largest community. It is a distribution centre for both western Manitoba and eastern Saskatchewan, and is the home of several significant manufacturing plants.

Many houses in Flin Flon are built on solid rock, and pipes are laid on the surface by adding protective wooden sleeves.

Population

Statistics Canada regards Greater Winnipeg as a census metropolitan area. In 1976 its population was 578 217, about 56 per cent of Manitoba's total of 1 021 056. Other cities had populations as follows:

Brandon	34 901
Thompson	17 291
Portage la Prairie	12 555
Flin Flon	8 152

WINNIPEG

Most of the world's major cities have grown as a result of one particular activity. Some owe their prominence to industry, some to transportation, some to government, and some to trade and commerce.

Winnipeg, however, has evolved through a bewildering tangle of complementary careers. Preceded by a fur trading post, it was founded as an agricultural settlement. Later it became triply important as a transportation centre, as Manitoba's seat of government, and as the commercial capital of Canada's midwest.

In the twentieth century, Winnipeg has blossomed as a manufacturing centre, as a bastion of education and culture, and as one of North America's leading convention cities. Manitoba has long been known as the keystone province, but perhaps Canada's real keystone is Winnipeg.

Because Winnipeg has never stopped growing, there are few reminders of its previous incarnations. The old stone gateway of Upper Fort Garry has been preserved, and Louis Riel's remains lie in a cemetery in St. Boniface. Otherwise, the most compelling reminders of the city's past are housed in the Manitoba Museum of Man and Nature.

The oldest inhabited buildings in Winnipeg date from the mid-nineteenth century, as does St. Andrews on the Red (1849), Western Canada's oldest stone church still in continuous use. The handsome legislative building on the banks of the Assiniboine river was completed as recently as 1919.

Apart from the legislative building, Winnipeg's most impressive feature is its modern architecture. Major midtown development projects have raised the Winnipeg skyline high above the flat prairie that surrounds it, but without neutralizing Winnipeg's special character.

The centre of Winnipeg is the junction of Portage Avenue and Main Street, as it has been since the days of the fur

Winnipeg's year is enlivened by a number of festivals, among them the carnival-style *Festival du Voyageur*, which is a reminder of the province's French heritage.

trade. Most of the major developments are located close by. Among them are hotels, office blocks, shopping malls, public buildings, and the Winnipeg Convention Centre.

Opened in 1975, the Convention Centre occupies a complete block of the downtown core. It contains a large open space available for meetings and exhibitions, a 600-seat movie theatre, stores, boutiques, and underground parking. The convention area can accommodate more than 7000 people at a time.

The convention 'industry' has become important in North America, and Winnipeg now bills itself 'Canada's Convention City.' It attracts provincial, national, and international gatherings, and adds muscle to Manitoba's hospitality and tourist industries. Delegates are encouraged to explore other parts of the province while they have the chance.

Another impressive complex is set on Main Street. On one side is Winnipeg's civic centre, two buildings housing the city council and the city administration respectively. Across the street are the Manitoba Museum of Man and Nature and the Manitoba Centennial Concert Hall.

The Manitoba Museum of Man and Nature, one of the most progressive in Canada, contains a rich series of exhibits covering Manitoba's past and present. One gallery holds a full-scale replica of Groseilliers's *Nonsuch*, whose voyage in 1669 led to the foundation of the Hudson's Bay Company.

The concert hall is the home of the Winnipeg Symphony Orchestra, and in fall and winter it accommodates the Royal Winnipeg Ballet for its subscription seasons. Elsewhere in the city the Winnipeg Art Gallery is a work of art in itself, and the Manitoba Theatre Centre is one of Canada's most respected regional theatres.

For outdoor recreation, Winnipeggers can turn to the city's many parks. Assiniboine Park is the largest, and includes a zoo. Kildonan Park is the site of the Rainbow Stage summer theatre. St. Vital Park has a large lake, which in winter provides Winnipeg's finest skating.

Sports enthusiasts frequent Winnipeg's 20 golf courses and 25 curling clubs, though the most impressive sports facilities are a legacy of the Pan American Games held in Winnipeg in 1967, notably the Pan Am Pool. Polo Park is the home of the city's two professional sports franchises, the Blue Bombers (football) and the Jets (hockey).

The impressive ruins of the sixth St. Boniface cathedral, like its predecessors destroyed by fire. A seventh cathedral has been built close by.

Christmas lights on Winnipeg's Portage Avenue, close to the heart of the city.

BUSINESS

At the centre of Winnipeg is the corner of Portage and Main, the heart of the city's business district. Close by is the Winnipeg Commodity Exchange, the most famous symbol of private enterprise in Western Canada.

The exchange was established in 1887, when a group of Winnipeg merchants organized premises where grain dealers, millers, and shippers could discuss their business. At first only cash transactions were recognized, those in which individual buyers and sellers negotiated each detail of their contracts.

In 1903 the exchange introduced the more speculative 'futures' market, the basis of most of its business today. Futures are contracts for future delivery, prepared by the seller and auctioned to the highest bidder. Such contracts specify quantity, quality, point of delivery, and the month delivery will be made.

In the first year only wheat futures were traded, but in 1904 oats and barley futures were added. Subsequently, all three were withdrawn from the open

market when the Canadian Wheat Board was made the sole marketing agency for prairie wheat, oats, and barley sold interprovincially or outside Canada.

Today, the exchange recognizes trading in rye, flax, and rapeseed futures on the international and domestic markets, and feed grades futures in wheat, oats, and barley on the domestic market alone. In addition, since 1972 it has provided facilities for futures trading in gold bullion, the only such market in Canada.

Like the exchange, the offices of the Canadian Wheat Board are close to Portage and Main. Foreshadowed by a similar organization set up during World War I, the Wheat Board was established by the Dominion government in 1935, to combat the instability of grain prices during the depression years.

At first, the Wheat Board's function was to guarantee a minimum price for wheat in competition with the open market. When prices were low, farmers and elevator operators could sell to the Wheat Board. When prices were higher

Clustered near the confluence of the Assiniboine (foreground) and Red rivers, Winnipeg is centred on the domed Legislative Building and the business district beyond.

than the minimum, they could sell on the open market, probably through the exchange.

That was the position until 1943, when trading in wheat futures was suspended as a war measure. The Wheat Board was granted powers concerning the whole prairie wheat market. When the war ended, the board was allowed to retain these powers, and in 1947 it was extended to cover oats and barley too.

Today, the Wheat Board markets prairie grain in about 80 countries. Many of its sales are negotiated by the board itself, but others are arranged by private trading companies acting as its export agents. Such companies also supervise the loading of grain cargoes leaving Canada, and sometimes assume responsibility for ocean freight.

On the prairies, individual farmers deliver grain to country elevators, ac-

cording to allotted quotas. Elevator operators act as agents of the Wheat Board and make initial payments to the farmers. The grain is held in the elevators until required for railing to the terminal elevators at Thunder Bay, Churchill, or Vancouver.

At the crop year's end, the Wheat Board makes a final payment to each producer, based on its total sales of the grade of grain he delivered. Throughout, the Wheat Board acts as entrepreneur on behalf of prairie farmers in general, and its operations are paid for by small deductions from the farmers' receipts.

Closely concerned with the fortunes of the international grain market are the two chief farm co-operatives based in Manitoba, the Manitoba Wheat Pool and United Grain Growers. Both have their head offices at Portage and Main. So has the Canadian Grain Commission, the Crown agency responsible for maintaining the standard of grain products destined for export.

Banks and insurance houses crowd close to the corner as well, and with them the offices of several of Winnipeg's manufacturing enterprises. A few blocks away is the most famous company of all. In 1970 the Hudson's Bay Company moved its head office to Winnipeg from London, exactly three centuries after receiving its charter to Rupert's Land.

For the company, the move to Winnipeg made sound business sense. Its operations within Canada are more widespread than those of any other enterprise, catering not only for the cities of the south, but for many scores of communities throughout the north. From Winnipeg, the company serves all parts of Canada and at the same time has speedy access to the United States.

Tourism has become a major factor in Manitoba's economy, particularly around Winnipeg. Among the capital's many attractions are pleasure cruises on the Red river, some of them travelling all the way to Lower Fort Garry.

The floor of the Winnipeg Commodity Exchange is at times the liveliest spot in Manitoba. Most of the exchange's business depends on futures trading in grain or gold bullion.

GOVERNMENT

For a decade after its formation in 1870, Manitoba consisted of little more than the Red river valley. It was known as 'the postage stamp province,' a reference to its rectangular shape and its lonely position on the map, far away from its neighbours.

As settlement spread, so did the province. In 1881 its northern boundary was extended to 51°50'N, its eastern boundary was redrawn to meet Ontario's new limits, and its western boundary was set close to its present interface with Saskatchewan, a province established in 1905.

Finally, in 1912 a major redistribution of what had been the North West Territories gave Manitoba access to Hudson Bay, and carried its northern boundary to the 60th parallel. Even so, all this time the Dominion government retained control of Manitoba's natural resources and did not surrender it until 1930.

Today, Manitoba sends 13 representatives to the House of Commons in Ottawa and has six seats in the Senate. For its part, the federal government appoints the province's lieutenant-governor and also the judges of Manitoba's superior courts, the Court of Queen's Bench and the Court of Appeal.

The lieutenant-governor heads the

Twin buffaloes dominate the steps leading to the legislative assembly chamber. A buffalo head is enshrined in Manitoba's coat-of-arms.

Close to the Legislative Building in Winnipeg is Manitoba's Superior Court, housed in the low courts building.

Government House in Winnipeg (left) is the official home of the province's lieutenant-governor. Close by is the Legislative Building.

provincial legislature, as representative of the Crown. His official home is 10 Kennedy Street in Winnipeg, a handsome building within a stone's throw of the legislative building on the banks of the Assiniboine. No bill can become law until the lieutenant-governor has signed it.

The other element of the legislature is the legislative assembly, which contains members elected from 57 ridings, about half of them in Winnipeg. Elections are called at intervals of no longer than five years. Following an election, the leader of the party which has won the most seats is invited by the lieutenant-governor to form a government.

The leader of the party becomes Manitoba's premier, and the members he chooses for his cabinet are sworn in as ministers of the Crown. Each is pledged to head branches of the provincial administration, which normally consists of about 15 departments active in matters within the province's jurisdiction, as well as assorted Crown agencies.

The fields in which the provincial government is active include educa-

tion, health, management of natural resources, and justice administration. In addition, the government supports agriculture and the arts, promotes industry, commerce, and tourism, and builds provincial highways and other public works. Manitoba's Crown agencies include the utilities supplying electricity, natural gas, and telephone services.

The third branch of the provincial government is the judiciary, consisting of the superior courts and a variety of lesser courts in which provincial judges preside. For judicial purposes the province is divided into five assize districts, each regularly visited by justices of the Court of Queen's Bench.

At municipal level, Manitoba has five incorporated cities, more than 30 incorporated towns, 40 incorporated villages, and more than 100 rural municipalities ranging in size from 4 to 22 townships, each township covering about 15 km². Each municipality is governed by a locally elected council.

By far the biggest of these municipalities is the City of Winnipeg, which contains more than half of Manitoba's population. Before 1972, Greater Winnipeg consisted of 12 independent municipalities, but in that year they came together as a single 'Unicity.'

Before the amalgamation, the various municipalities offered widely differing standards of service, depending on

their resources. Now, the same standards are applied throughout Winnipeg. 'Unicity' is divided into 29 wards, each electing a representative to the city council, and the councillors elect the mayor.

When founded in 1870, Manitoba was known as the 'postage stamp province,' because on the map it looked like a stamp on an envelope. In 1881 its size was increased, and after 1912 its boundaries were extended to reach the 60th parallel.

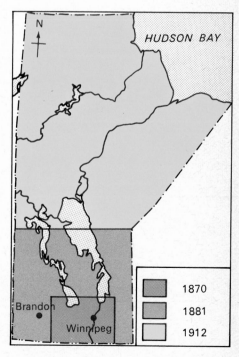

THE LEGISLATURE

In 1911 Manitoba's legislators decided to erect a new legislative building. They wanted a structure 'not for present delight or use alone, but such as our descendants will thank us for.'

An architectural competition was conducted throughout the British Empire, and the design selected as winner was by Frank Worthington of Liverpool, England. Excavations on the site in Winnipeg began in 1913, and the building was completed in 1919. The legislature first sat in it in 1920.

Ever since, the legislative building has been the focal point of Winnipeg and of all Manitoba. Built in the shape of an H and surmounted by a massive dome, it is set in immaculately kept gardens sloping gently to the Assiniboine river. On top of the dome is Manitoba's most famous landmark, the Golden Boy.

Created by the French sculptor Charles Gardet during World War I, the Golden Boy clutches a sheaf of wheat in his left arm and holds up a lighted torch. He faces north, and represents the spirit of progress advancing towards new frontiers.

Gardet also sculpted the two bronze buffalo that flank the grand staircase within the building. The stairs and the floor are of marble, but the building as a whole is constructed of limestone from the Tyndall quarries outside Winnipeg.

Filled with towering columns and classical motifs, the interior carries strong reminders of ancient civilizations.

In the heart of the building is the legislative chamber, with members' desks arranged in the shape of a horseshoe around the speaker's chair. The chair doubles as a throne when the lieutenant-governor is present — for instance, when he is opening a session of the legislature.

Today, the lieutenant-governor's role in the legislature and administration is largely formal, but it was not always so. For several years following the creation of Manitoba in 1870, the lieutenant-governor was the chief political influence in the province.

Before the first election, held in December 1870, lieutenant-governor Adams Archibald ruled by proclamation, when necessary following directives from the governor-general in Ottawa. Following the election, Archibald appointed an executive council or cabinet from members of the legislative assembly. No premier was chosen, though some historians claim that other members of the council recognized Alfred Boyd as their leader. It was Archibald who presided at council meetings.

Archibald's successor, Alexander Morris, continued to preside over or join in council meetings until 1876, though he did appoint a premier, Marc Girard, in 1874. Since 1876 the premier has

Manitoba's legislative assembly in session. The assembly consists of 57 members, who elect a speaker from their own number to preside over their deliberations.

presided over meetings of his cabinet without interference from the lieutenant-governor.

Party politics evolved slowly in Manitoba. Members of the legislative assembly tended to follow the lead of federal politicians active in Ottawa, but not until 1900 was a recognizable political party elected to office. The provincial Conservatives had campaigned on a platform of economy and efficiency and an end to the public sale of liquor.

It was the Conservatives who introduced plans to construct the legislative building. Construction started, but soon there was a scandal. Substantial overpayments were revealed, and in the election of 1915 the Conservatives were beaten by the Liberals.

After the election of 1920 the Liberals remained the largest party in the assembly, but were outnumbered by members of other parties. There was another election in 1922, and on that occasion the United Farmers of Manitoba won 27 of 53 seats. However, the group had no party organization and no leader, and most of them were only interested in their constituents. Even so, the farmers were persuaded to form a

The Premiers

Officially, Manitoba's first premier was Marc Girard, appointed in 1874. But some historians insist that the executive council had earlier recognized Alfred Boyd, Girard, and H. J. H. Clarke as 'first among equals.'

Before 1900 there were no party politics in Manitoba, but since then Conservatives (C), Liberals (L), United Farmers (UF), Progressive Conservatives (PC), and New Democrats (NDP) have formed administrations. From 1928 until 1958 Manitoba was served by coalition governments (coal.).

The premiers of Manitoba have served as follows:

Roblin

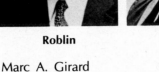
Weir

Schreyer

Lyon

Marc A. Girard	1974	John Bracken (UF)	1922-1928
Robert A. Davis	1874-1878	John Bracken (coal.)	1928-1943
John Norquay	1878-1887	Stuart S. Garson (coal.)	1943-1948
D. H. Harrison	1887-1888	D. L. Campbell (coal.)	1948-1958
Thomas Greenway	1888-1900	Duff Roblin (PC)	1958–1967
H. J. Macdonald	1900	Walter Weir (PC)	1967–1969
Rodmond Roblin (C)	1900-1915	Edward Schreyer (NDP)	1969–1977
T. C. Norris (L)	1915-1922	Sterling Lyon (PC)	1977–

government, but by 1928 they had had enough of politics and resigned.

There followed a succession of coalition governments that continued until 1958. During World War II Liberals, Progressives, Conservatives, the CCF, and the Social Credit party came together. In 1945 the CCF members withdrew from the coalition, and in 1958 the Conservatives also broke away and won 26 seats against the coalition's 19 and the CCF's 11.

For the first time in 30 years Manitoba returned to party government, with Duff Roblin as premier. In 1959 the Conservatives won a clear majority. Throughout the 1960s Conservative and Liberal support was eroded by the New Democratic Party, which was formed when the CCF joined forces with organized labour.

The swing from right to left could not have been more extreme. During eight years in office, the NDP introduced wide-ranging social reforms and expanded government activity in the private sector. In 1977 the pendulum swung again, and they were defeated by the Conservatives, who forthwith set about reducing the size of the government and the extent of its commitments.

The dome of the legislative building is surmounted by the 'Golden Boy,' Manitoba's most famous landmark. The statue represents the spirit of progress advancing towards the north.

EDUCATION

One of the first acts of the NDP government elected in 1969 was to guarantee Franco-Manitobans the right to education in the French language. The decision provided a happy ending to a dilemma that had troubled successive administrations for the best part of a century.

When Manitoba joined Confederation in 1870, its few schools were in the hands of church groups. Seventeen were operated by Roman Catholics, fourteen by Anglicans, and two by Presbyterians. Under the Manitoba Act, French was recognized as an official language, and most of the Roman Catholic schools offered instruction in that tongue.

The Manitoba Act expressly guaranteed the survival of denominational schools, whether Protestant or Catholic,

Story-telling in the library of an elementary school in Winnipeg. At most schools tuition is in English, but at some it is in French, catering to true Franco-Manitobans or to English-speaking students involved in an immersion course.

Universities

Early Manitobans' ethnic and religious differences gave rise to several special colleges representing the points of view of their founders. In 1877 three of the most prominent colleges came together as the University of Manitoba in Winnipeg.

The founding colleges were St. Boniface (French-medium and Roman Catholic), St. John's (Anglican), and Manitoba College (Presbyterian). They were joined by Manitoba Medical College in 1882, the Methodist church's Wesley College in 1888, the Manitoba College of Pharmacy in 1902, and the Manitoba Agricultural College in 1906.

Yet more colleges joined later, but in 1967 the process was reversed. Colleges of the University of Manitoba were reconstituted as universities in their own right. United College (the former Manitoba College and Wesley College combined) became the University of Winnipeg, and Brandon College (which had joined the University of Manitoba in 1938) became Brandon University.

Both Winnipeg and Brandon universities are relatively small, offering a limited number of undergraduate programs. The University of Manitoba, on the other hand, is one of the largest in Canada. Among its leading faculties are those of agriculture, architecture, dentistry, education, engineering, law, medicine, and science.

Brandon University was originally a college of the University of Winnipeg, but became independent in 1967.

as did an amendment to the British North America Act. Accordingly, the first Manitoba School Act passed in 1871 provided for a dual system of schools, Catholic and Protestant, administered by local trustees responsible to a provincial board of education.

Instruction was offered in English or French as appropriate, and from 1873 in German, too — a concession to German-speaking Mennonites. However, a flood of English-speaking Protestant settlers, particularly from Ontario, swiftly changed the population balance so that Franco-Manitobans were a small minority.

During the late 1880s, there were demands for a unitary system of public schools, on the principle that a single large school could be equipped with better facilities and more proficient staff than two small ones. At the same time there was agitation against Roman Catholics in general, and particularly against the French.

In 1890 the government of the day abolished the official use of French in Manitoba, and also the dual school system and the status of denominational schools in general. A provincial Department of Education was set up, and English became the sole language of education.

Inevitably there were protests. Led by Archbishop A. A. Taché of St. Boniface, the French of Manitoba took the issue to the courts. Frustrated in Manitoba, they went to Ottawa. There the federal government split on the issue and the Conservative prime minister, Mackenzie Bowell, was forced to resign.

In 1897 the federal Liberals came to power, and persuaded the Liberal government of Manitoba to accept a compromise. Where a minority group was large enough and when parents requested it, Roman Catholic (or non-Roman Catholic, if the minority was Protestant) staff were to be appointed. Under the same conditions, religious instruction might be given at the end of the school day. These provisions remain in force.

Another element of the compromise affected language rights. Where numbers warranted, French-speaking students or those speaking other languages were to be taught in their own tongue as well as in English. The provision was designed to benefit not only the French, but also the Mennonites, who demanded that their children be taught in German.

Before long, the immigration boom that brought tens of thousands of Europeans to Canada's west was under way. Not French and Mennonites alone, but Ukrainians, Poles, and other groups demanded instruction in their own language. In most cases the privilege was granted, even when the teachers concerned were poorly qualified to in-struct in their first language, let alone in English.

The province tried to overcome the problem by setting up French, Ukrainian, and Polish normal schools to train teachers, but their impact was small. During World War I, patriotic Manitobans suggested that the linguistic diversity threatened Canada's future as a unified nation. In 1916 the provincial government abolished bilingual teaching, leaving English as the sole language of instruction in all Manitoba schools.

That was the position until 1970, when the NDP turned back the clock to the situation of a century before. Franco-Manitobans now have their own schools, though they usually make extensive use of English as well as French. Many of the 'English' schools in Manitoba reciprocate by offering immersion courses in French.

Both English- and French-medium schools are organized in 47 school divisions administered by elected school boards, operating under the general supervision of the province's Department of Education. Nine remote schools are administered separately, and six schools for Indians are governed by trustees appointed by the department.

Students at a public school work on individual projects. Schools in Manitoba are organized in 47 school divisions, each administered by an elected school board.

HOSPITALS

In Winnipeg, amalgamation for the sake of efficiency has become a tradition. In 1973, 12 neighbouring municipalities joined forces as Unicity, and in the same year four of the city's hospitals were united as the Health Sciences Centre.

The largest single component of the centre is what used to be the Winnipeg General Hospital, which was established in 1872. At first it was housed in a room above a drug store on Main Street, but soon it expanded into rented accommodation elsewhere in the city.

In 1875 a tract of land was donated to the hospital, and as years passed the

The Health Sciences Centre of Winnipeg, which includes Manitoba's largest referral hospital and a number of specialist institutions. Close by is the University of Manitoba's Faculty of Medicine.

Halloween in the child life playroom at the Health Sciences Centre. Some children must spend a considerable time in hospital, and staff try to make their stay happy.

General gathered strength. From 1883 its efforts were supplemented by those of Manitoba Medical College, the nucleus of today's faculty of medicine at the University of Manitoba. The General's school of nursing was founded in 1887.

Today, the General is known as General Centre. One of its wings, founded in 1950 as the Women's Pavilion, is now a separate hospital for women, known as the Women's Centre. The two institutions are the chief referral hospitals in Manitoba, and together serve as the major training ground for medical students at the university.

A third component of the Health Sciences Centre used to be Winnipeg's Children's Hospital, founded in 1909. At first it was accommodated in a dilapidated house bought for the purpose, but it soon outgrew its cramped quarters and moved to new premises. The Children's Centre, its current home, was built in 1956.

The Rehabilitation and Respiratory Centres are descended from a small isolation hospital founded in Ninette in 1910. The sanatorium was intended to care for those suffering from tuberculosis, the dangerously infectious disease that was then the chief killer of people aged between 15 and 60.

There was steady expansion of the sanatorium's facilities, but more and more sufferers were being discovered. A clinic was established in Winnipeg itself, and in the 1940s and 1950s new programs were devised to help patients recover from the effects of tuberculosis. Later, these rehabilitation programs were extended to those suffering from disabilities of other sorts.

Tuberculosis is much less of a menace than it used to be, and its place has been taken by cancer. The Manitoba Cancer Treatment and Research Foundation, an affiliate of the Health Sciences Centre, had its roots in a private institution established in 1930. In 1957 the foundation was made responsible for professional and scientific cancer control throughout Manitoba.

Increasingly, hospitals seek to treat patients at home. Patients benefit from greater mobility, and hospitals can make their beds available to those who need them. Here a home care nurse instructs a patient in the use of portable oxygen equipment.

Drug dispensing at the touch of a button. The method is swift and accurate, and helps pharmacists to fill prescriptions without delay.

Other hospitals in the province tend to be overshadowed by the Health Sciences Centre, but several maintain close links with it. The centre co-operates with other Winnipeg referral hospitals like St. Boniface and Misericordia, and with the Grace Hospital, Manitoba's leading maternity institution.

For health administration purposes, Manitoba as a whole is divided into seven health regions, each equipped with at least one referral hospital. Those at Brandon, Dauphin, and The Pas are especially well equipped. There are also more than 80 small community hospitals providing short-term primary care.

In northern Manitoba, there are modern hospitals in centres like Churchill and Thompson and, in addition, a number of federal nursing stations attached to Indian reserves. Patients requiring special treatment are usually flown to Winnipeg.

Manitoba's hospitals have always been a source of local pride, and even

today neighbouring communities often prefer to operate separate establishments, rather than combine their resources on a single location. The result is that hospital expenses outside Winnipeg are generally higher than they need to be.

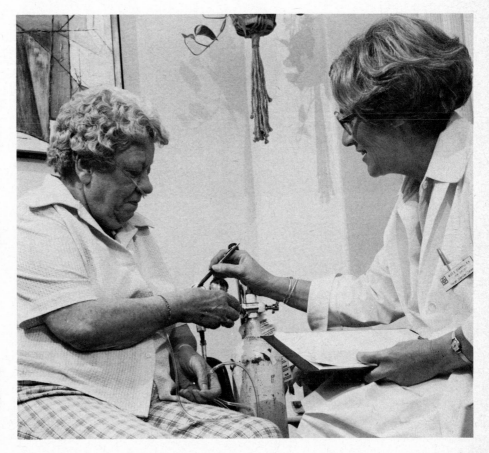

Dancers of the Royal Winnipeg Ballet warm up before a performance. Founded in 1938, the ballet has become world famous and is one of Manitoba's most valued assets.

Each summer, Winnipeg's Rainbow Stage performs open-air musicals under an enormous dome in Kildonan Park.

PERFORMING ARTS

The four cornerstones of the performing arts are theatre, symphony music, ballet, and opera. All four are well represented in Manitoba, three of them by professional institutions famous throughout Canada.

Theatre in the province is dominated by the Manitoba Theatre Centre, one of Canada's leading regional theatres. Housed in impressive quarters in Winnipeg, the centre stages six plays a year, each running for three weeks. Periodically, productions staged at the centre tour the province.

Le Cercle Molière, based in St. Boniface, is one of Canada's most accomplished French-language theatres, founded in 1925 and believed to be the oldest operating theatre group in the country. *Le Cercle* presents three major productions each year, and is based at the Franco-Manitoban Cultural Centre in St. Boniface.

Throughout summer, the Rainbow Stage in Winnipeg provides a season of open-air musicals, staged under a dome in Kildonan Park. Experimental theatre flourishes at the Manitoba Theatre Workshop in Winnipeg, which offers tuition in all aspects of drama and stages innovative productions at its own in-house theatre.

The Winnipeg Symphony Orchestra, one of Canada's most important, made its debut in 1948. It has been organized on a professional basis since 1958, and today offers fall and winter subscription series at Winnipeg's Centennial Concert Hall. In addition it broadcasts frequently.

Even better known is the Royal Winnipeg Ballet, which acquired its royal title in 1953 following a command performance before Queen Elizabeth II. Founded in 1938, the ballet offers fall and winter subscription series in Winnipeg and Brandon, and each year performs open-air ballet in Winnipeg's Assiniboine Park.

The ballet regularly tours Canada and the United States, and occasionally performs outside North America. Attached to it is a major ballet school. Complementing the company's work are Winnipeg's Contemporary Dancers, a modern dance troupe formed in 1970 that has won an enthusiastic following.

The Manitoba Opera Association, largely amateur, stages three operas each year, and is particularly well supported by New Canadians. The opera is helped by a strong choral tradition in Manitoba, not least the work of the Mennonite Children's Choir of Winnipeg, which is one of the finest of its kind in North America.

It is not out of place to mention a fifth element in Manitoba's performing arts, the world of rock and roll. Winnipeg produced the Guess Who, which achieved world fame in the 1960s, and its offshoot Bachman Turner Overdrive (B.T.O.) which proved almost as successful. The 'Winnipeg Sound' became familiar on six continents.

The Winnipeg Symphony Orchestra has been professional since 1958, and offers regular subscription series in Winnipeg's Centennial Concert Hall.

Books and Paintings

A number of Canada's leading writers are native Manitobans, though most of them have long since left the province. The best known are Gabrielle Roy and Margaret Laurence.

Gabrielle Roy was born in St. Boniface and educated in Winnipeg, and for a time taught in prairie schools. She later wrote of prairie life in such novels as *La Petite Poule d'Eau* (1950), translated as *Where Nests The Water Hen,* and the semi - autobiographical *Rue Deschembault* (1955), translated as *Street of Riches.* She now lives in Montreal.

Margaret Laurence was born in Neepawa, and she too was educated in Winnipeg, though she now lives in Ontario. Several of her novels describe life in 'Manawaka,' a fictional prairie community not unlike Neepawa.

Native Manitobans among Canada's non-fiction writers include the critic George Woodcock, who now lives in British Columbia; James Gray, a popular historian, now in Alberta; and the oral historian Barry Broadfoot, who now lives on Vancouver Island.

The exodus of Manitoba's contemporary talent contrasts with the situation late in the nineteenth century, when there was an invasion of writers from Ontario. Among them was Nellie McClung, whose family homesteaded near Brandon in the 1880s. Nellie McClung's novels won her influence

and respect that helped her to promote the cause of women's rights.

Another Ontarian writer was C. W. Gordon, better known as 'Ralph Connor.' Appointed pastor of a church in Winnipeg, 'Connor' wrote such books as *Glengarry Schooldays* (1902), which made him the best-selling Canadian author of his generation. For several years Frederick Philip Grove, Canada's first realistic novelist, lived in Manitoba, and his accounts of prairie life in the pioneer years have great documentary value.

The best - known painter to emerge from Manitoba was Lionel LeMoyne Fitzgerald of Winnipeg, who joined Ontario's Group of Seven in 1932. A year later he was a founding member of the Canadian Group of Painters, as was Charles Comfort, who had studied at the Winnipeg School of Art.

L. L. Fitzgerald's painting *Pritchard's Fence* **(1928). In 1932 Fitzgerald became a member of Ontario's Group of Seven.**

Art Gallery of Ontario

SPORT AND RECREATION

In 1967, more than 3000 leading athletes from North, Central, and South America took part in the Pan American Games held in Winnipeg. To celebrate the event, the city built an Olympic pool, a velodrome (for cyclists), and a track and field stadium.

The games introduced Manitobans to a wide range of sports not previously popular in the province, and left Winnipeg with sports facilities among the finest in Canada. Even so, they did little to change a deep-rooted Manitoban idea that intensely competitive sport should take place indoors, while the open air should be used for rest and relaxation.

A result of this idea is that most competitive sport takes place in the winter months. Hockey and curling attract tens of thousands of enthusiasts, and few communities are without twin arenas. Where ice-making equipment is available, the arenas are in use for up to

Manitoba's long-standing connections with Scotland are reflected in two of the province's most popular sports, golf and curling. The annual curling bonspiel in Winnipeg is regarded as one of North America's most prestigious.

eight or nine months of the year.

The highlight of Manitoba's curling season is the annual bonspiel in Winnipeg, organized by the Manitoba Curling Association. Regarded as one of the world's most prestigious, it attracts more than 700 rinks from all over North America and occasionally from Europe, too. Significantly, prize money is modest. Competitors take part for the honour of winning, rather than with hopes of rich rewards.

In Winnipeg, basketball and volleyball have both become popular. They, too, are indoor sports. Outdoor team sports like soccer (particularly in Winnipeg) and baseball (particularly in the Brandon area) are played more for fun than with a keen competitive urge.

Recreational activities popular in the province range from the simple to the sophisticated. Many Winnipeggers are content to jog or cycle in summer, and to skate or ski cross-country in winter. Tennis is popular and golf even more so — Manitoba has more courses per head of population than any other province. For winter sports enthusiasts, there are several downhill ski runs.

Perhaps the most distinctive recreational pursuits depend on water. With so many rivers and lakes available, Mani-

tobans are keen canoeists and fishermen, and in recent years the northern two-thirds of the province have come into their own as Manitobans and visitors have explored their potential. Sport fishing takes place not only in summer, but also in winter, when anglers jig for whitefish through holes in the ice.

The Winnipeg Rowing Club, active on the Red river, is one of Western Canada's oldest sports associations. On Lake Winnipeg, Pan American Games facilities developed at Gimli are being utilized by Manitoba's yachtsmen, who sail a large fleet containing both dinghies and keelboats. There is more fine sailing on Lake of the Woods.

Winnipeggers support two professional sports franchises, one playing Canadian football and the other hockey. The football players are the Winnipeg Blue Bombers, formed in the 1930s and in 1935 the first team from Western Canada to win the Grey Cup. In one period they won the cup four times in five years (1958, 1959, 1961, and 1962).

The Winnipeg Jets were among the founding franchises of the World Hockey Association, which had its first season in 1972-1973. Paced by the veteran star Bobby Hull, the Jets have been one

Duck and goose hunting have long been favourite pastimes in Manitoba, particularly as migrating waterfowl can seriously damage farmers' crops.

of the league's most successful teams, and in 1976 and 1978 won the Avco Cup, the WHA's equivalent of the National Hockey League's Stanley Cup.

Rodeo is not as popular in Manitoba as it has become farther west, but the annual Manitoba Stampede at Morris is the biggest in the province. Where Calgarians wear white hats, Morris stampeders wear red. Another significant rodeo is organized at Swan River, and smaller events are organized to coincide with local fairs and festivals.

Sports apart, Manitobans make good use of their leisure time in cultural pursuits. Libraries and museums — particularly the Manitoba Museum of Man and Nature in Winnipeg — are well supported. Choirs, drama groups, and clubs and societies of all kinds are active in all parts of the province. Together, these influences help Manitobans to take good care not only of their physical health, but of their social and mental well-being, too.

A party of cross-country skiers in Turtle Mountain provincial park. Today's Manitobans enjoy outdoor winter sports as much as they do those of summer.

Folklorama

Manitoba's busiest festival takes place in Winnipeg in August, and is lively enough to entice native Winnipeggers back from their beach cottages. Known as Folklorama, it consists of upwards of 30 mini-celebrations staged by ethnic groups representing the city's many communities.

Each group organizes a pavilion representing the country of its ancestors, and in most cases named after that country's leading city. At the pavilion the group offers appropriate food and entertainment, and night after night for a week its members do what

At Winnipeg's Folklorama, singers and dancers of the Dutch community perform at the Amsterdam pavilion in the style of their forefathers.

they can to make their guests feel that they are far from home.

Pavilions are located all over Winnipeg, linked by a free bus service. Visitors gain access by means of a special passport, and most people aim to take in several pavilions in an evening. That way they can enjoy an aperitif in Tokyo, dinner in Beirut, and a stage show in the Caribbean, and still have time for a nightcap in Dublin or Amsterdam.

FESTIVALS

Each July, farmers and steam tractor afficionados from across Manitoba gather in Austin for the annual Threshermen's Reunion. Stooking and bag-tying contests, tractor pulls, and a rodeo keep old skills alive and preserve the memories of decades past.

The Threshermen's Reunion is one of several dozen such events that highlight the social calendar of rural Manitoba. Large or small, serious or frivolous, the local festivals enable Manitobans to celebrate their origins and learn more about each other, and at the same time help visitors to appreciate Manitoba's remarkable diversity.

Several of the festivals are associated with a particular ethnic group. One of the largest is Canada's National Ukrainian Festival in Dauphin, held at the end of July. Participants dress in traditional costume, and music, dancing, arts and crafts, and good food are prominent.

Similar ingredients are present at other ethnic celebrations, among them the Icelandic Festival at Gimli on Lake Winnipeg, where residents of the inter-lake region recall their Viking ancestry. Scottish Manitobans play pipes and drums at the Manitoba Highland Gathering at Selkirk, while Mennonites organize the Steinbach Pioneer Days and play a leading part in Altona's Sunflower Festival.

Like Quebeckers, Franco-Manitobans mark the festival of St. Jean Baptiste. One of the biggest gatherings is at La Broquerie, where participants dance in the streets and sing traditional songs. Another Franco-Manitoban celebration is the *Festival du Voyageur*, a winter carnival in St. Boniface.

Indians of the Big Eddy reserve near The Pas celebrate Opasquia Indian Days, when near-forgotten aspects of their heritage are recalled. During York Boat Days at Norway House, Indians and Métis from a wide area race flat-bottomed craft like those manned by their forefathers in the days of the fur trade.

Manitoba's biggest ethnic celebration is at Dauphin, the home of Canada's National Ukrainian Festival. Dancers, singers, cooks, and crafts producers join forces to keep Ukrainian traditions alive.

One of the most popular events on Manitoba's calendar is the Northern Manitoba Trappers' Festival at The Pas, held early in February. The highlight of the festival is the world championship dog derby, which attracts contestants from across Canada and from the United States too. Teams must travel about 220 km over three days.

Mining skills are honoured during Nickel Days in Thompson, when miners forsake the darkness of the working face to test their prowess in the full light of day. Flin Flon's Trout Festival features a 240 km Gold Rush canoe derby over the surrounding lakes and rivers, contested by two-man crews, and also a major fishing contest.

Corn and apples are celebrated at Morden in August, and beef and barley at Russell in October. In March, Churchillians celebrate the Aurora Snow Festival, and in July the Minnedosa Country Fun Festival includes a Railroaders' Day, recalling the contribution of railways to the prairie way of life. In Beausejour, a winter carnival in February coincides with the North American Power Toboggan Championships.

A major folk music festival is organized in Winnipeg, but most of Manitoba's arts festivals are designed for participants more than for spectators. The Holiday Festival of the Arts in Neepawa offers workshops in painting, music, dance, and drama. The International Music Camp at the Peace Gardens south of Boissevain attracts young

Chuckwagons race past the crowded grandstand at the Manitoba Stampede in Morris, one of Canada's most important rodeos.

people from Canada and the United States.

The round of festivals is completed by three which cater to zanier tastes. Canada's only mule derby is held in conjunction with the Miami agricultural fair. Frog Follies at St. Pierre feature the Canadian jumping frog championship. At Boissevain, competitors from across the country gather to contest the Canadian Turtle Derby.

A stooking contest at the Threshermen's Reunion in Austin. Another feature of the festival is an impressive parade of vintage steam engines.

PARKS AND GARDENS

One day in July 1932 more than 50 000 people from all parts of Canada and the United States gathered in the hills near Turtle Mountain, south of Boissevain. They were attending the opening of the world's largest garden dedicated to peace.

The site selected for the garden straddled Manitoba's border with North Dakota, close to the geographic centre of North America. A plaque erected to commemorate the opening bore the

Hecla provincial park is set on a number of islands in the middle of Lake Winnipeg, the largest of them connected with the mainland by a causeway.

inscription, 'To God In His Glory, We Two Nations Dedicate This Garden, And Pledge Ourselves That As Long As Men Shall Live, We Will Not Take Up Arms Against One Another.'

The plaque still stands, and each year many thousands of visitors make a pilgrimage to the International Peace Garden to honour the pledge. Lakes, terraces, formal flower beds, and an arboretum add to the garden's natural beauty, and provide a perfect setting for the annual music camp attended by young people from Canada and the United States.

The garden is not the oldest of Manitoba's public parks. That distinction belongs to Assiniboine Park, long since absorbed by the City of Winnipeg though it was originally set in open countryside. The park contains an important zoo, a large conservatory, formal flower gardens, and wide green lawns equipped with playing fields and bicycle paths.

The oldest provincial park, and also the largest and most used, is the Whiteshell in eastern Manitoba. Established in 1962, the Whiteshell offers lakes and forests in the setting of the Precambrian Shield. Crater Lake, believed to have been formed by a meteorite, is Manitoba's deepest.

Across the province and west of Lake Winnipegosis is the Duck Mountain provincial park, situated on the Manitoba Escarpment — not to be confused with a park similarly named in Saskatchewan. The park holds several dozen glacial lakes notable for fine fishing. It is also the home of a major herd of elk, whose high-pitched mating call can be heard in early fall.

North of The Pas is the Clearwater Lake provincial park, famous for trout fishing. The lake is also notable for nesting waterfowl and big game, especially moose. Closer to Flin Flon is the Grass River park, one of the wilderness areas in Manitoba's park system. It contains several groups of woodland caribou.

The other provincial parks in Manitoba are much smaller, but each has been developed to preserve a unique geographic feature, such as the shifting

Fishermen take their ease on a lake in the Whiteshell, Manitoba's oldest provincial park.

sand dunes of Spruce Hills, or to make the most of recreational possibilities. Grand Beach and Hecla parks on Lake Winnipeg fall into the latter category.

Altogether there are 11 provincial parks in Manitoba, as well as 10 provincial forest reserves in which visitors are welcome, and 44 small recreation areas. The park system provides wide variety in canoe routes, hiking trails, cross-country ski trails, snowmobile trails, and some of the finest fishing in Canada.

The only national park in Manitoba is at Riding Mountain at the edge of the Manitoba Escarpment. The slopes of Mount Agassiz on the park's eastern flank are steep enough to reward downhill skiers, but most of Riding Mountain is a gently rolling plateau studded by lakes and forests.

Much of the activity at Riding Mountain centres on Clear Lake, the park's most extensive stretch of water, and the resort community of Wasagaming, which has a golf course and swimming and boating facilities. Elsewhere in the park there are hiking and nature trails and also bridle paths.

Manitoba has two national historic parks. One is Fort Prince of Wales, at Churchill, where the fortifications partly destroyed by a French squadron in 1782 have been restored. The second is Lower Fort Garry, north of Winnipeg, where construction started in 1830. Today the fort makes a picturesque destination for the pleasure steamwheelers that cruise the Red river.

Canadian and American flags fly in the International Peace Garden that straddles the international border near Turtle Mountain. The garden was opened in 1932.

Wildlife

Most bear species sleep through winter and come alive in spring and summer. The polar bear's schedule is the reverse. Its busiest season is winter, when it ventures on to sea ice in pursuit of seals, its favourite prey.

In spring when the ice melts, the bears go ashore, grazing on vegetation and doing what they can to escape the heat of the sun. Males return to the ice as soon as it forms, but pregnant females remain ashore and dig complex maternity dens in deep snowbanks. One of the world's largest denning areas is located south of Churchill, and there is another east of the mouth of the Nelson river.

Churchill is close to the migration route used by many younger male bears making for the sea in fall, and each year bears searching for food pose a major problem for conservation officers there. When possible, marauders are scared off. If they are too persistent, conservation officers livetrap and tranquilize them, then release them far from the town.

Black bear, moose, and elk are all indigenous to Manitoba, and so are woodland caribou. Two herds of barren land caribou migrate south into Manitoba from the Northwest Territories. The white-tailed deer was unknown in Manitoba a century ago, but has spread with settlement until today it is the most common big game species.

Fur-bearers like beaver and muskrat are plentiful in northern Manitoba, and the arctic fox is found along the coast of Hudson Bay. There are wolverines and timber wolves in the boreal forest, and small colonies of prairie dogs survive in the grasslands. Badgers, porcupines, red foxes, and skunks add to the variety.

Manitoba is located on three of the four north-south flight corridors used by migratory waterfowl in spring and fall. More than 35 species of geese and ducks are commonly seen in Manitoba, among them Canada geese and snow geese. Many of the geese breed on the Hudson Bay flatlands, and other species nest in the marshes south of Lakes Winnipeg and Manitoba.

At Narcisse in the Interlake region there are six limestone pits that serve as winter homes for upwards of 20 000 garter snakes. In late April the snakes emerge from their winter sleep, and soon entwine themselves in tangled 'mating balls,' each containing dozens of males attracted to a single female. The snakes disperse for the summer, then recongregate in fall.

The world's largest polar bear denning grounds are located close to Churchill, and bears come close to the town in fall as they make their way to the ice forming on Hudson Bay.

Manitoba's fortunes rose as the buffalo herds declined. The buffalo's head is enshrined on Manitoba's coat-of-arms.

THE BUFFALO

Early Spanish visitors to North America described it as 'nothing but cows and sky.' The 'cows' were buffalo or, more properly, North American bison, tens of millions of animals that crowded the plains of the interior.

In what is now Manitoba, Indian tribes hunted the plains buffalo for meat, hides, and bowstrings. With the growth of the fur trade, buffalo hunting became an industry, as Indians, Métis, and white hunters slaughtered animals in hundreds of thousands. No other species was so useful to man in so many different ways.

Before the nineteenth century, there were probably between 50 million and 60 million plains buffalo in North America. By 1830 the number was down to about 40 million. By 1885, the species was faced with extinction. In 1893, the Canadian government moved to protect the few hundred animals that survived on Canadian soil.

The Canadian herd was amplified by animals introduced from the United States, and by interbreeding with the more plentiful wood buffalo of the north and west. Today, the position of plains buffalo is relatively strong. Among Canada's herds is one in Riding Mountain National Park.

Manitoba owes much to the buffalo, and the province has recognized its debt in a charming way. The animal is enshrined in Manitoba's coat of arms, a lasting reminder that the mighty bison gave the province its start, and that its inevitable decline before the advance of settlement allowed Manitoba to rise from its bones.

Thousands of buffalo once roamed throughout Manitoba's grasslands, but only a few small herds survive. This one is in Riding Mountain National Park.

Photograph Credits

Health Sciences Centre: p. 52 top and bottom, p. 53 top and bottom; *Irvin Kroeker*: p. 7 top; *Manitoba Department of Agriculture*: p. 23 top and bottom, p. 25 bottom; *Manitoba Department of Mines, Natural Resources, and Environment*: p. 29 bottom; *Manitoba Government Travel*: p. 3, p. 4 top and bottom, p. 6 bottom, p. 7 bottom, p. 10 bottom, p. 11 top and bottom, p. 14 bottom, p. 18 bottom, p. 19, p. 22 top, p. 25 top, p. 26, p. 27 top, p. 28 top, p. 29 top, p. 33 top, p. 36 bottom, p. 37 top, p. 37 bottom, p. 39 top and bottom, p. 42, p. 43 top and bottom, p. 44, p. 45 top and bottom, p. 47 top, p. 49 top row and bottom, p. 50 bottom, p. 54 top and bottom, p. 55 top, p. 56, p. 57 top and bottom, p. 58 top and bottom, p. 59 top and bottom, p. 60 top and bottom, p. 61 top and bottom, p. 62 top and bottom; *Manitoba Provincial Archives*: p. 14 top, p. 16 bottom, p. 17 top, p. 20 top and bottom, p. 21 top and bottom; *Manitoba Public Information*: p. 24, p. 27 bottom, p. 30 top and bottom, p. 31, p. 32 top and bottom, p. 33 bottom, p. 35 bottom, p. 36 top, p. 38 top, p. 40, p. 41 top and bottom, p. 46 top and bottom, p. 48; *Winnipeg School Board*: p. 50 top, p. 51.

Acknowledgments

Many individuals, corporations, institutions, and government departments assisted us in gathering information and illustrations. Among them we owe special thanks to the following:

Air Canada
Canadian Government Office of Tourism
Canadian National Railways
CP Rail
Canadian Wheat Board
City of Winnipeg
Crystal Springs Hutterite Colony
Folklorama
Freshwater Fish Marketing Corporation
Health Sciences Centre
Hudson Bay Mining and Smelting Company
Hudson's Bay Company
Inco Limited
Terry Kolodaychuk
Irvin Kroeker
Lower Fort Garry National Historic Park

Dennis Maksymetz
Manitoba Archives
Manitoba Chamber of Commerce
Manitoba Department of Agriculture
Manitoba Department of Economic Development
Manitoba Department of Education
Manitoba Department of Mines, Natural Resources, and Environment
Manitoba Department of Municipal Affairs
Manitoba Department of Tourism and Cultural Affairs
Manitoba Farm Bureau
Manitoba Forest Resources
Manitoba Health Organizations Incorporated
Manitoba Hydro
Manitoba Pool Elevators
Manitoba Public Information Services

Manitoba Stampede
Manitoba Theatre Centre
Mennonite Village Museum
Mining Association of Manitoba
Pasta of Winnipeg
Public Archives of Canada
Royal Winnipeg Ballet
Sherritt Gordon Mines
United Grain Growers
University of Manitoba
VIA Rail Canada
Winnipeg Blue Bombers
Winnipeg Economic Development Board
Winnipeg Commodity Exchange

If we have unwittingly infringed copyright in any photograph reproduced in this publication, we tender our sincere apologies and will be glad of the opportunity, upon being satisfied as to the owner's title, to pay an appropriate fee as if we had been able to obtain prior permission.

Canadian Cataloguing in Publication Data

Hocking, Anthony, 1944-
  Manitoba

(Canada series)

Includes index.
ISBN 0-07-082688-9

1. Manitoba.   2. Manitoba — Description and travel.
I. Series.

FC3361.6.H63   971.27   C77-001606-5
F1062.5.H63

Index

CANADIAN STATISTICS

	Joined Confed-eration	Capital	Area	Population (1976)	Ethnic Origin (% 1971)		
					British	French	Other
CANADA		Ottawa	9 976 185 km²	22 992 604	45	29	26
Newfoundland	1949	St. John's	404 519 km²	557 725	94	3	3
Prince Edward Island	1873	Charlottetown	5 657 km²	118 229	83	14	3
Nova Scotia	1867	Halifax	55 491 km²	828 571	77	10	13
New Brunswick	1867	Fredericton	74 437 km²	677 250	58	37	5
Quebec	1867	Quebec City	1 540 687 km²	6 234 445	11	79	10
Ontario	1867	Toronto	1 068 587 km²	8 264 465	59	10	31
Manitoba	1870	Winnipeg	650 090 km²	1 021 506	42	9	49
Saskatchewan	1905	Regina	651 903 km²	921 323	42	6	52
Alberta	1905	Edmonton	661 188 km²	1 838 037	47	6	47
British Columbia	1871	Victoria	948 600 km²	2 466 608	58	4	38
Yukon	—	Whitehorse	536 327 km²	21 836	49	7	56
Northwest Territories	—	Yellowknife	3 379 699 km²	42 609	25	7	68